# Needle Tatting For Complete Beginners

Adrianna .G Robbins

All rights reserved. Copyright © 2023 Adrianna .G Robbins

# COPYRIGHT © 2023 Adrianna .G Robbins

All rights reserved.

No part of this book must be reproduced, stored in a retrieval system, or shared by any means, electronic, mechanical, photocopying, recording, or otherwise, without written permission from the publisher.

Every precaution has been taken in the preparation of this book; still the publisher and author assume no responsibility for errors or omissions. Nor do they assume any liability for damages resulting from the use of the information contained herein.

**Legal Notice:**

This book is copyright protected and is only meant for your individual use. You are not allowed to amend, distribute, sell, use, quote or paraphrase any of its part without the written consent of the author or publisher.

# Introduction

This is a comprehensive guide that delves into the art of needle tatting, offering a detailed background to help readers understand the craft's origins and significance. The tutorial and pattern section serves as a practical hands-on approach, guiding beginners through the process of tatting with needles, emphasizing the creation of rings joined by needle tatting.

The guide then provides valuable insights into the fundamental techniques of needle tatting, focusing on the intricate steps involved in making rings and picots. This foundational knowledge serves as a basis for the subsequent sections, enabling readers to progress with confidence.

For those interested in practical applications, the guide explores necklace tatting with a needle, demonstrating how the acquired skills can be applied to create beautiful and wearable pieces of art. The step-by-step instructions and visual aids make it accessible for beginners to embark on their tatting journey.

Understanding how to use a needle for tatting is a crucial aspect covered in detail, ensuring that readers are equipped with the necessary skills to navigate the craft effectively. The guide goes beyond basics, providing a hands-on approach to learning needlework through the creation of a flower pendant.

Aspiring needle tatters can further expand their repertoire with the tatted-winged angel project, offering a more intricate pattern to challenge and enhance their skills. The needle tatting pattern section provides additional creative avenues, encouraging readers to explore the craft independently.

This book stands out as a valuable resource, catering to novices keen on unraveling the art of needle tatting. By combining background information, practical tutorials, and engaging projects, the guide ensures a holistic learning experience for those venturing into the captivating world of needle tatting.

# Contents

CHAPTER ONE NEEDLE TATTING BACKGROUNG ...................................................1
CHAPTER TWO TUTORIAL AND PATTERN: TATTING WITH NEEDLES ................11
CHAPTER THREE RINGS JOINED BY NEEDLE TATTING ......................................32
   HOW TO TAT: HOW TO MAKE RINGS AND PICOTS.............................................41
CHAPTER SIX NECKLACE TATTING WITH A NEEDLE ..........................................71
   HOW TO USE A NEEDLE FOR TATTING ...............................................................98
CHAPTER EIGHT LEARN NEEDLEWORK USING MY FLOWER PENDANT .........109
CHAPTER NINE TATTED-WINGED ANGEL ..........................................................123
CHAPTER TEN NEEDLE TATTING PATTERN .......................................................133

# CHAPTER ONE NEEDLE TATTING BACKGROUNG

Tatting was significant to M. Marie Grauer. Grauer, who was born in Marysville on June 15, 1895, served as a teacher at Marysville High School, gave piano lessons, and eventually worked as a secretary.

She compiled tatting samples and directions into a pattern book. She wore a tatted wristlet to carry the ball of thread while working with the tatting shuttle. Grauer tatted a variety of household items, including bedding and towels. Grauer passed away in Marysville on

May 17, 1991. Many of her tatting supplies were donated by her family to the Kansas Historical Society.

Tatting has its origins in ancient Egypt and China. Popular in Europe throughout the 18th century, immigrants introduced the art to America, where it gained popularity. is an ancient craft. It is a technique for creating lace by looping and knotting a single thread strand on a small shuttle. It has been nicknamed "beggars lace" because to the fact that it can be created from remnants of virtually any smooth thread.

Tatting is a method utilized to create lace. Using loops and knots, a long tatting needle or shuttle can be used to form rings and trains. Tatting can be performed with both crochet yarn and AISA brand, which has a silky smooth texture. The higher the thread count, the more delicate the thread. The thread size also influences the size of the pattern.. When selecting a thread, it is necessary to consider the project at hand. Consider the item's frequency of use; for instance, Easter-themed decorative trims will only be used once a year, whereas collars and handkerchiefs will be worn and laundered frequently. Tatting can be used to create a variety of objects, including doilies, earrings, necklaces, home decor, collars, etc.

**Initial steps you must master**

• Master the double Stitch

• Establish a Double-Stitch Chain

• Learn how to create rings

• Study how to produce picots

**Materials needed**

• Material

• Vehicle

• Needle

• Cutters

**Varieties of Tatting:**

• **Needle Tatting** - Like knitting, needle tatting is a form of needlework. The size of the project is determined by the size of the needle. The finer the thread required, the smaller the needle. Shuttle tatting is more stable than needle tatting due to the usage of imitation rings in needle tatting.

- **Shuttle Tatting** - This was the first technique used to create tatted lace. The shuttle guides the wound thread through a loop to create knots.

**Cro-tatting** is a blend of crochet and needle tatting. A tatting needle with a crochet hook is utilized.

## Abbreviations Used in Embroidery

If you need inspiration for tatting, you can discover tatting books and instructions online or in bookstores. To read tatting instructions, it is necessary to be familiar with the often used abbreviations, such as beg for beginning chain and sm p for small picot. Visit Lovely Tatting for a comprehensive list of tatting acronyms.

## Shuttle Tatting For Beginners

This is a wonderful instructional video for novice tatters. It clearly and effectively demonstrates the fundamental procedures required to master tatting. The audience is instructed on how to thread and wind a shuttle, construct a double stitch, and open and close a ring. All of these skills must be mastered before beginning a tatting project.

## Needle Tatting for Beginners

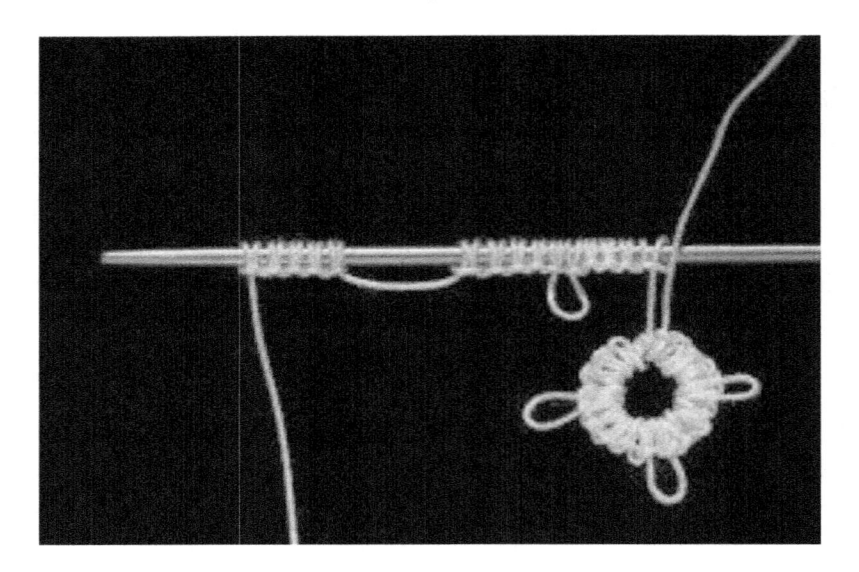

Needle tatting will be right up your alley if you knit. This tutorial is a step-by-step instruction to the fundamental skills of needle tatting. The Thread Corner explains each process completely and efficiently, making them simple to comprehend and follow. Check out her channel for other useful tatting advice.

Once you have mastered the fundamentals, it is time to move on to more complex tasks. Frivole provides a full lesson on how to tatt a crystal star if you wish to expand your artistic horizons. Check out the numerous creative and instructive tatting videos available online. Remember that the more you practice, the quicker and simpler it will become.

**Benefits**

Tatting is beneficial to health. The rhythmic motion can alleviate anxiety, irritation, and restlessness by acting as a stress reliever. Knitting and crocheting are additional crafts with comparable benefits.

## Helpful Tips

• To unwind a thread, suspend the shuttle and the thread will unwind itself.

Always ensure that the thread is wound evenly. Do not extend thread past the edge of the shuttle.

• For a neat appearance, secure loose thread ends on the incorrect side of the project.

• Tatted Treasures has additional helpful tatting tips.

## Needle or shuttle when learning to tat?

Tatting is something I've always wanted to learn. I adore the way that this lovely type of lace looks. But which should I master first, shuttle or needle? These two techniques' final appearance may be similar, but their implementation differs. Simple implements like thread, scissors, a crochet hook, and a needle or shuttle are needed.

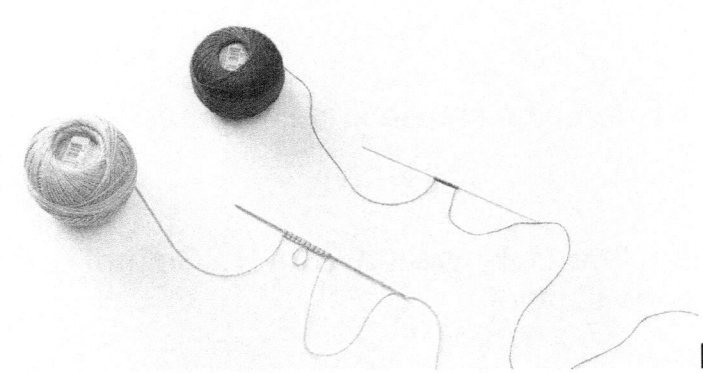

Double stitch in closeup.

Most people think that needle tatting is the simpler of the two methods. Different sizes of needles and threads are paired according in part to their diameter. The needles are lengthy and have a consistent thickness from tip to eye. I'm reminded of the kindergarten cast-on in knitting when I begin a double stitch on a tatting needle. Although the stitches are tightly stitched on the fine needle, their fineness is limited by the needle that was employed. There are more ends to weave in during needle tatting because a shorter length of thread is used. Additionally, one must take care to prevent thread abrasion from stitching-related friction. However, needle tatting is a wonderful option when the lace needs to be decorated because beads can be added more easily.

plastic shuttles for tatting.

Conversely, shuttle tatting doesn't require a needle. As fine as the thread gauge being utilized, you can work. Shuttles come in a wide range of sizes, forms, and materials, including plastic, wood, and metal. Additionally, shuttles can handle more thread, which means there are fewer ends to weave in. Although shuttle tatting can first feel difficult, with practice, both hands can move the shuttle and thread in a coordinated manner to produce elaborate and delicate rings and picots. In her shuttle tatting video, Georgia Seitz ingeniously demonstrates the fundamental stitch known as "the flip," a technique that frequently frustrates new tatters, using black-and-white shoelaces.

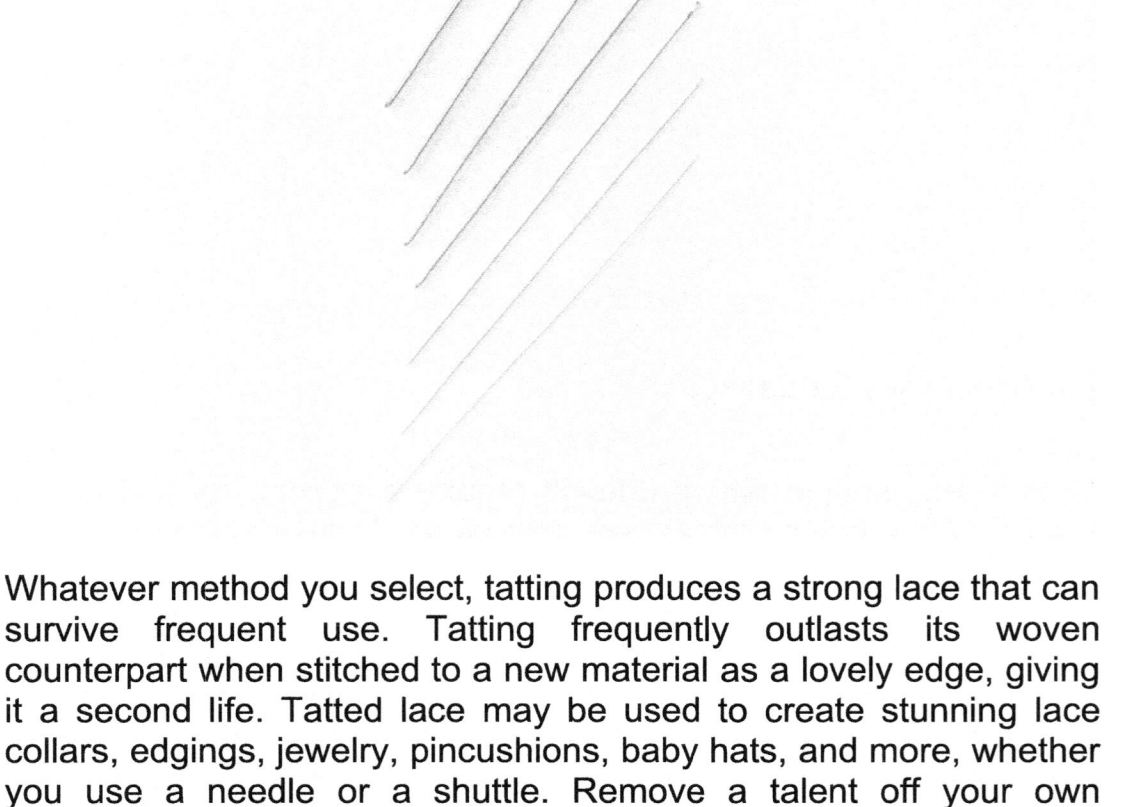

Whatever method you select, tatting produces a strong lace that can survive frequent use. Tatting frequently outlasts its woven counterpart when stitched to a new material as a lovely edge, giving it a second life. Tatted lace may be used to create stunning lace collars, edgings, jewelry, pincushions, baby hats, and more, whether you use a needle or a shuttle. Remove a talent off your own needlework wish list.

# CHAPTER TWO TUTORIAL AND PATTERN: TATTING WITH NEEDLES

Simple headband with tats

The goal of this is to introduce the fundamentals of needle tatting through a hybrid pattern and lesson. The headband is to be fashioned out of embroidery floss and is attractive. If headbands are not your thing, try making a bookmark or something similar. The pattern should still work for you if you prefer shuttle tatting and are not interested in needle tatting.

Despite the fact that this is meant to be the very beginning of tatting, I find the craft to be somewhat challenging to master (although very easy once you have). If you've already dabbled in fiber arts and know how to knit, crochet, sew, or do something similar, you should be fine. If you've ever been good at making the friendship bracelets that many camps teach, you'll also be fine. If you've never tried fiber arts before, you might want to start with something simpler. In my opinion, crochet is a great place to start.

**You will require:**

• 4 skeins of floss for embroidery (2 would be plenty for a bookmark). When you start larger projects, you might opt to use crochet threads instead of embroidery floss because they are more expensive but have a wider variety of sizes, colors, and fiber contents. Choose colors that work nicely together since your headband will display all four skeins of floss (see the four hues of blue above).

• 4 cards, bobbins, or spools of embroidery floss. These frequently come with variety packs of floss; if you don't have any, you may construct your own out of cardstock by cutting out a roughly 1" by 2" square and cutting slits in one end that will grab the floss. Alternatively, you can use empty thread spools or bobbins. The unused floss should simply be neatly coiled and out of the way.

• Sizes #5 and #3 tatting needles (the #3 is not required for a bookmark). I suggest purchasing a variety pack from your preferred craft retailer or searching online for a pack similar to this.

• It's not necessary, but it's nice to have a little (size E or smaller) crochet hook on hand.

• This may assist, but you don't need it if you have tiny hair clips, alligator clips, or something similar that is 3/8" to 1/2" broad.

**Setup:**

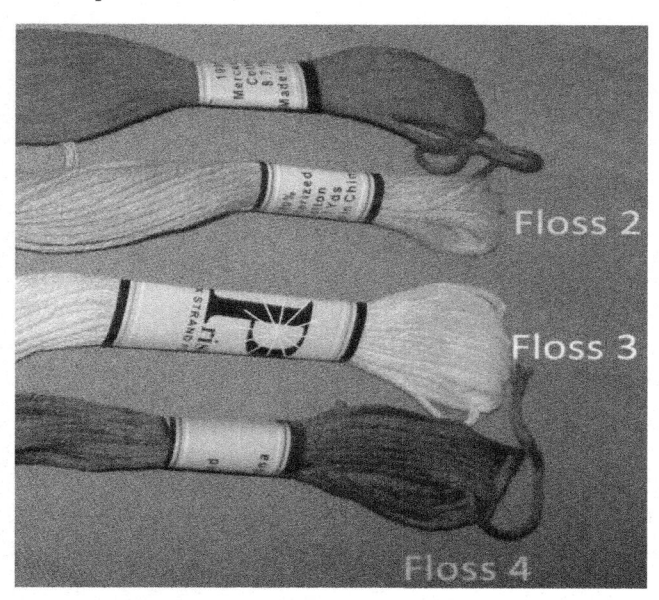

1. Choose the placement of your floss skeins. Count them from 1 near the front of your head to 4 toward the back.

2. Untangle skeins 1 and 2; be sure to do this on a broad, flat surface to avoid becoming hopelessly twisted. Try your best to

position the knot at the midpoint of the two skeins when you join them. I tie both threads together with one overhand knot.

3. Spool the two threads that are on one side of the knot. Wind floss number one onto a different spool on the other side of the knot, beginning at one end and winding in the direction of the knot. It is easier to manage the thread if the tail is nearly half the length of the thread. Thread floss number two onto your #5 needle. Your "ball thread" or "spool thread" is now floss 1, and your "needle thread" or "working thread" is floss 2.

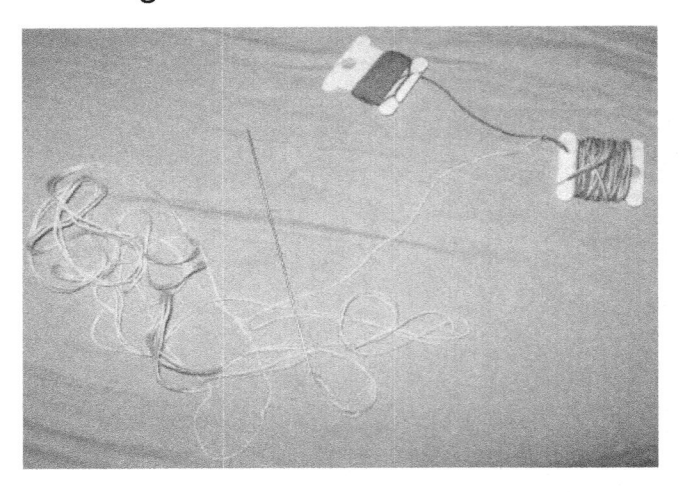

Some fundamental tatting theories or an overview: Nearly all tatting patterns are made out of "rings" and "chains" on a vast scale, with some higher level designs including clunky leaves, Josephine knots, etc. Rings and chains are precisely what they sound like: they are resembling circles where the thread enters and departs at the same spot, and they move the thread from one point to another. Tatting allows you to create almost any pattern that you can draw on paper without using a pen and without crossing too many times (loops are acceptable but nested loops are not).

Tatted rings and chains are created by repeating the double stitch, often known as a "ds," in which one thread is wrapped around another core thread. Picots and joins can be used to provide some structure and ornamentation. Picots are merely loops of thread that protrude from the row of stitches, while joins let you to connect a previously produced picot to a ring or chain. Although there are many lovely patterns employing picots of various lengths or with beads attached for adornment, I nearly solely use picots for joining. Making all of your picots the same size is a goal to aspire for while starting to tat; this requires a lot of practice (or using gauge tools).

**Step 1: Ring the bell**

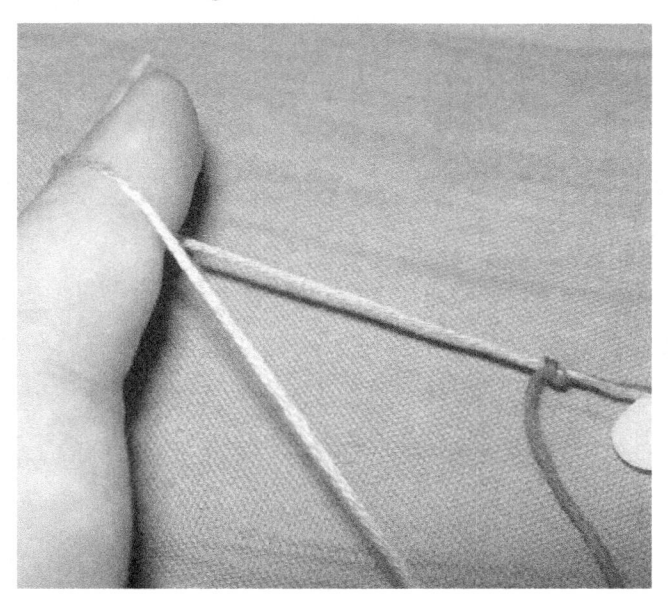

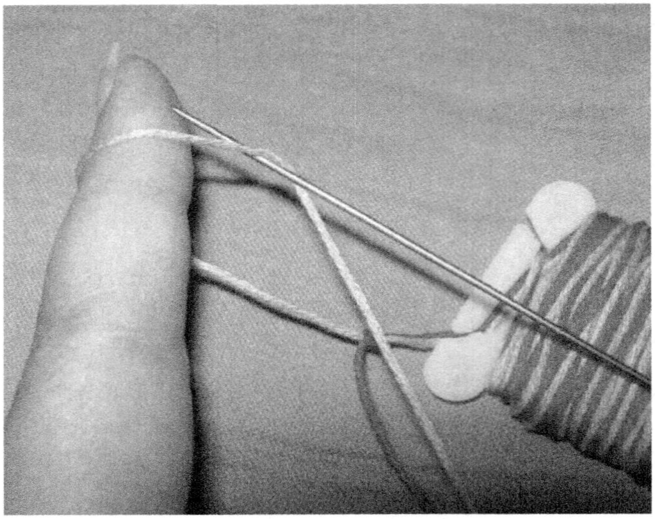

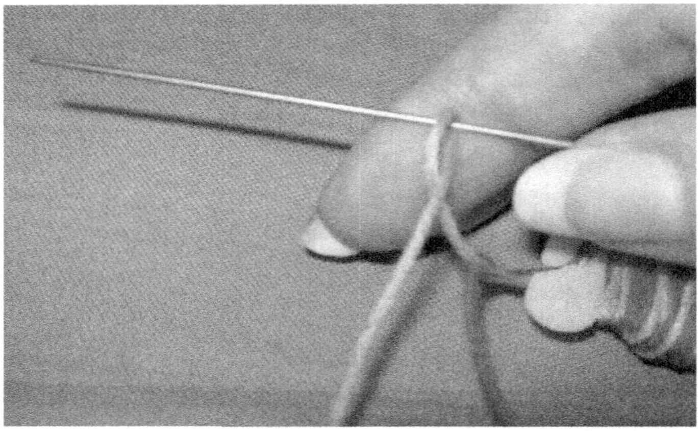

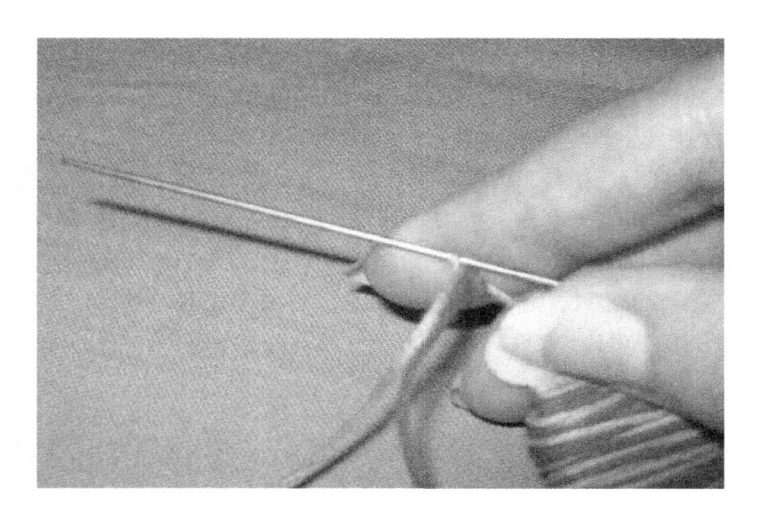

Making the initial half-hitch is step two.

1. With your right hand, hold the needle. To maintain track of the knot, press one finger against the needle's side. Keep your first finger free as you hold the working thread in your left hand about 6 inches from the knot, with the knot end held between your thumb and middle finger and the trailing end (facing the needle) going through your pinky.

2. Bend the working thread by positioning your first finger behind it, between your hand and the knot (see photos). Bring the needle up between the two sides of the working thread, under the front strand of the thread, and in front of it. Pull snugly as you slide your finger out of the working thread and use your left hand to push the stitch that has just been produced down the needle to the knot. The working thread should be caught under a loop of thread that crosses the needle, forming a half-hitch. Your very first stitch is here. Your right hand's first finger should be pressed up against the needle to secure it.

3. Reverse the procedure by bending your first finger backwards from in front of the working thread. Bring the needle up between the two sides of the thread, under, and behind the working thread's back strand. Pull the second stitch snugly against the first one after removing your finger. This is referred to as a cow hitch around the needle because it is a second half-hitch created with the opposite handedness of the previous one. This is known as a double stitch in tatting, or "ds" in pattern abbreviation.

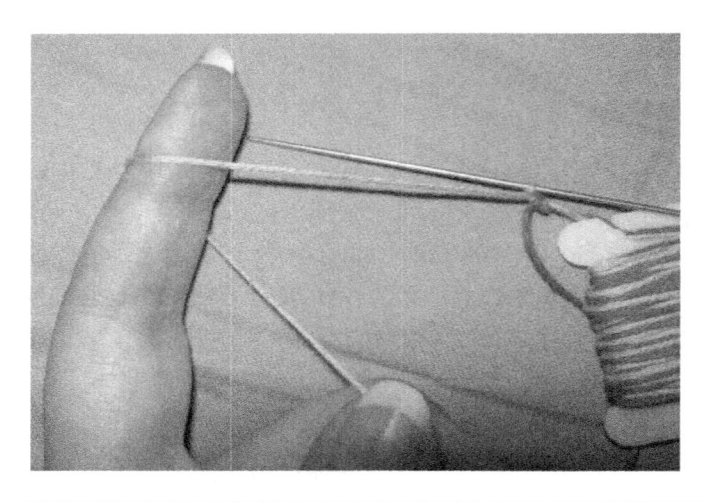

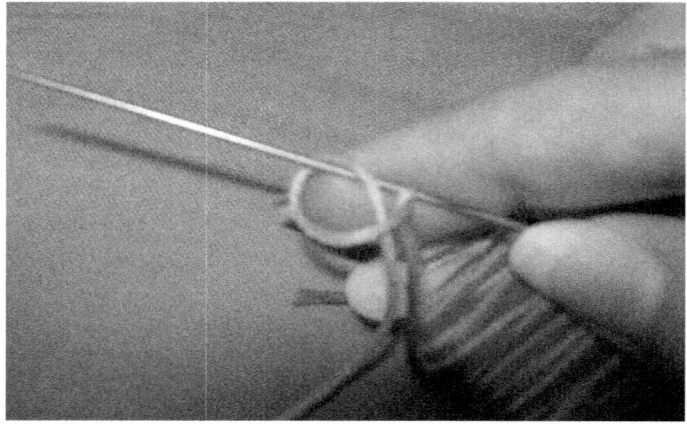

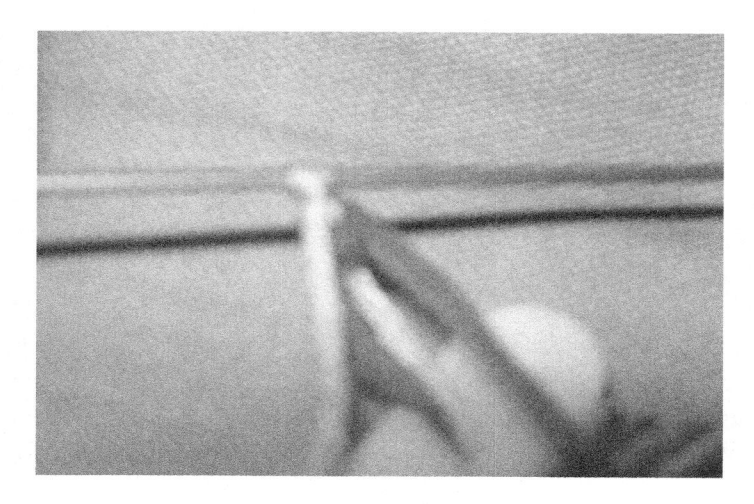

4.

For a total of 8 ds on the needle, repeat steps 2 and 3 a total of seven more times each (total of 16 single stitches).

5. It's time for your first picot, which is simply a space between stitches on the needle. Make your first single stitch as in step 2, but instead of pulling it tight against the stitch before it, leave a 3/8- to 1/2-inch gap between them by using the first finger of your right hand. If you have a 3/8" hair clip or something such, you can slide it onto the needle prior to sewing and hold it with the teeth facing away from the needle (see photo) to reinforce the gap. Then, pull the stitch snugly against it. Make sure you can remove it by unclipping, that is, without slipping any stitches off the needle, but leave it in place until you've added a few more stitches to hold the picot in place.

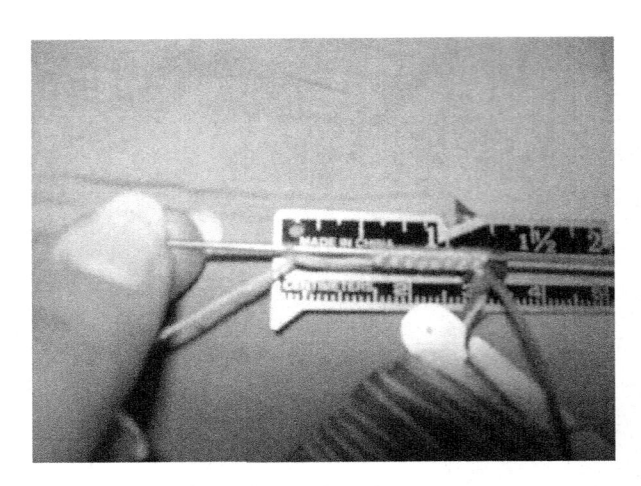

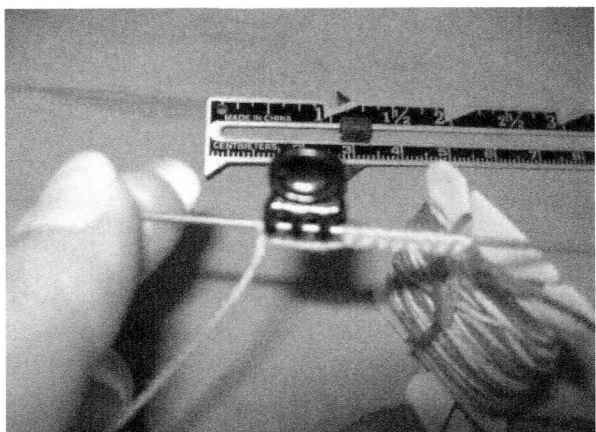

Whether using a tool or not, picot making

6. Create 7 more ds after completing the first set of ds by producing a single stitch as in step 3.

7.

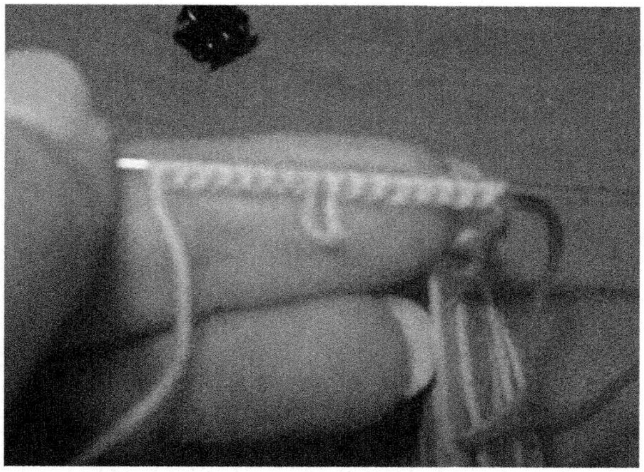

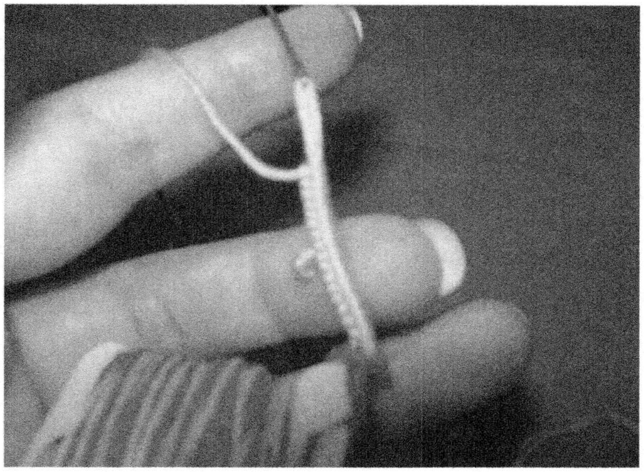

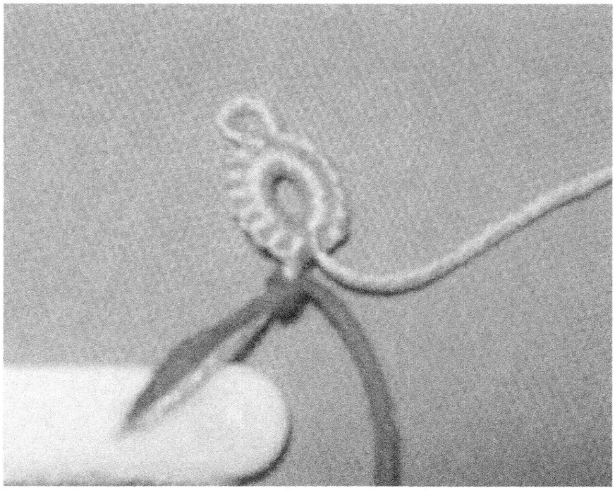

Picot closure and ring completion

Slide the new 8ds around the needle until they are adjacent to the previous 8ds while holding the last few stitches you made in your left hand. The thread for the picot should fold up into a loop that protrudes from the stitches.

8. Keeping all of the stitches together, continue to slide the needle with all of the stitches toward the eye. When the needle thread naturally draws the stitches into a loop with the picot and the bumpy parts of the threads on the outside, gently move the stitches from the needle onto the needle thread. Keep other threads out of the way in front of the closing loop, such as the ball thread and the needle thread that you've previously pulled through.

9. You've finished creating your first tatted ring. In a design, this would be written as "Ring: 8ds, picot, 8ds," "Ring 8-8," or "R8p8" depending on how succinct the notation is. This is because there are 8 double stitches on each side of a picot.

**Complete the motif.**

1.

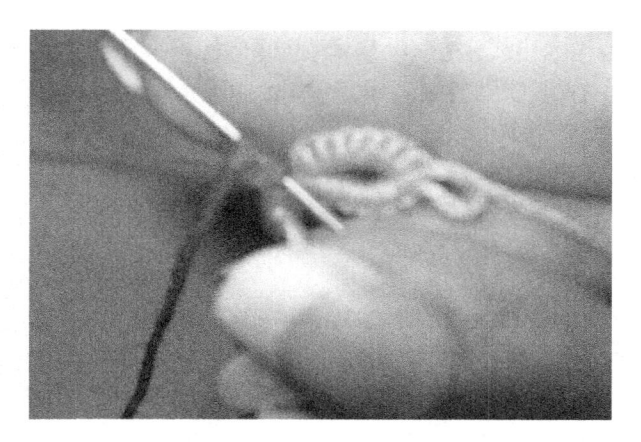

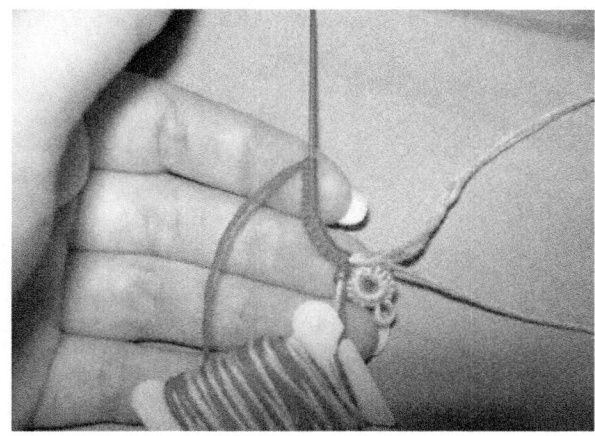

producing the chain

Hold the starting knot against the needle with your right hand once more while you turn the work so that the ring you just created is pointing up and the ball thread is pointing down. Similar to how you held the working thread earlier, hold the ball thread with your left hand.

2. Make 16 double stitches in a row using the ball thread.

3. Thread the needle with these stitches and pull it through; this time, the stitch won't form a ring but will instead naturally curve with the bumpy side of the stitch on the outside. You would write "Chain: 16ds" or "Chain 16" or "C16" in a pattern to indicate that this is your first chain.

4. Rotate the work so that the ring is pointing downward once more; then, place the end of the chain you just created against the needle so that the ball thread is above the working thread and hold the working thread in your left hand as you did with the last ring.

5. Sew 8 double rows.

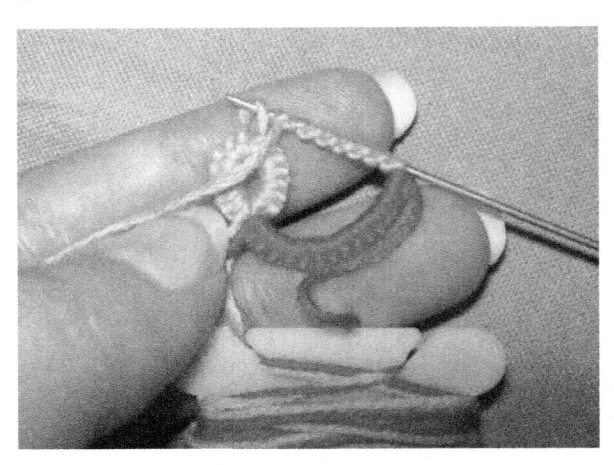

6.

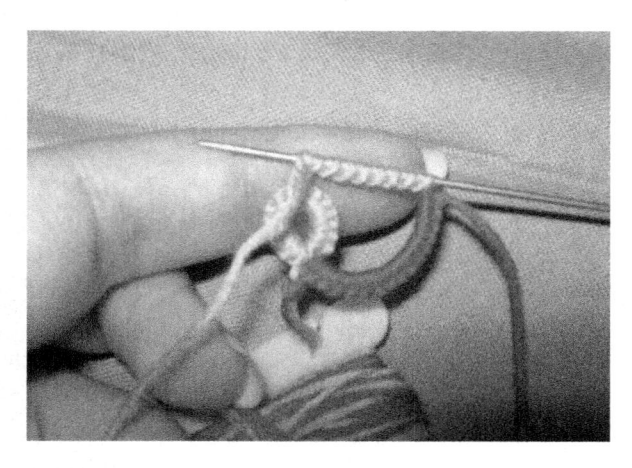

assembling the join

When it's time to connect the rings, draw the first one down and around until the picot is just at the tip of the needle, then slide the stitches you've already created forward on the needle until there is only about 1/4" of the needle tip left before the stitches.

7. Place your hand on the working thread and face the first ring. Right to left and back to front, thread the needle's tip through the picot. With the picot still on the needle, make a first single stitch and

draw it tightly against the preceding stitches. Pull the picot from the needle without removing the stitch by pulling it up and over the stitch you just made with your fingers or a little crochet hook. This is quite difficult to master; to make it simpler, move the stitches closer or farther away from the needle tip as necessary. If joining pieces together is proving to be too tough, you can skip the whole inserting the needle through the picot process and simply draw a loop of thread from front to back through the picot, forming it as a stitch on the needle.

8. Work the second single stitch, followed by 7 more double stitches to finish with 16 double stitches on the needle, half of which will be used for the join.

9. Continue to slide the stitches onto the thread of the needle, then pull them into a ring. Ring: 8ds, join (to picot of previous ring), 8ds, often known as "R8j8." The picot/join should be securely positioned at the center of the two rings, which should be the same size.

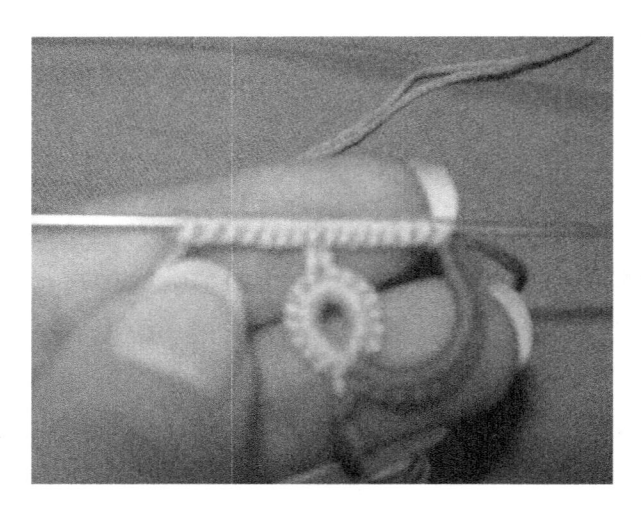

## Steps: Reducing motif size

1. Repetition of the previous stages, but with each set of eight missing one ds Ring: 7ds, picot, 7ds, in other words. 14d chain 7ds ring, join, 7ds. Consider this a "7-motif" in comparison to your initial "8-motif" ring-chain-ring design.

2. Create a second 7-motif by ringing 7d, picoting 7d, chaining 14d, and ringing 7d, joining 7d.

3. Create two six-motifs: (Ring 6ds, picot, 6ds; chain 12ds; ring 6ds, join, 6ds)*2.

Make two five-motifs (Ring 5ds, picot, 5ds; chain 10ds; ring 5ds, join, 5ds)*2.

5. Leave at least 8" of floss 2 for the tie and create two 4-motifs (or however many you have thread for).

6. Chain 6ds and leave the ends dangling for the time being.

Return to the initial knot and thread floss 2 onto your needle to create a bookmark. With floss 1, chain 16 double chains. Pull the floss taut and, for symmetry, tie another knot. Use floss 1 for floss 4 and floss 2 for floss 3, then skip to step 3 below. After step 6 below, tie the ends of all four threads together, clip the extra threads, and you're done!

**The remainder of the lace**

1. Make one 8-motif, two 7-motifs, two 6-motifs, two 5-motifs, and two 4-motifs (or however many you made on the other side), finishing with a chain of 6ds. 2. Repeat all of the steps above on the opposite side of the starting knot.

2. Unwind floss 3 and 4 and reassemble as you did at the beginning; floss 4 will serve as your working thread and floss 3 as your ball thread.

3. Begin a ring with 8ds using your working thread. Join this ring into the picot of an 8-motif by aligning the completed (floss 1&2) piece and the new work so that the knots are parallel (one that you have already used to join). To make the picot more accessible, you might want to use a needle or crochet hook. Just slip the needle into the picot and pull the outer edge away from the motif, slapping the ring that has already been linked there against the other one. Be careful not to twist anything because it should lie flat when the join is done. With 8 ds, complete the ring, then remove the needle and tighten.

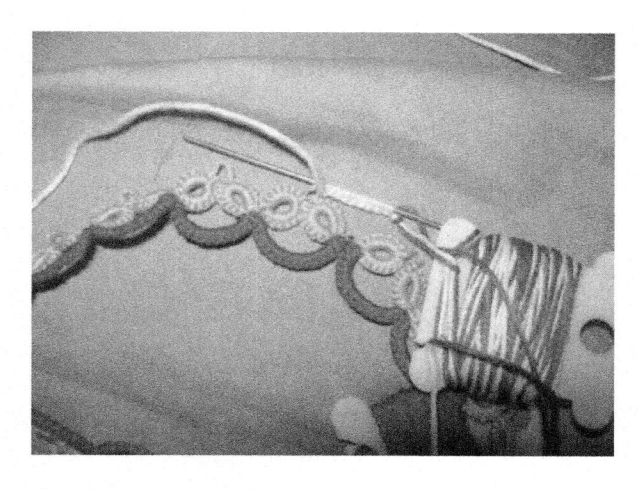

4. Chain 15 chains, join into the same picot you just joined into, and then chain 8 chains more to complete the modified 8-motif that is connected to the other piece. To accommodate the form of the skull, the chain is intentionally one ds shorter on one side than it was on the other. If you're producing a bookmark, chain 16 double stitches (ds) and work all of your designs as usual.

5. Continue by joining two modified 7-motifs to the 7-motifs in the first piece with the following instructions: (chain 13ds; ring 7ds, join, 7ds) twice.

6. Add two modified 6-motifs, two modified 5-motifs, and two modified 4-motifs to finish the pattern (or as many as you made before). The chains should be, respectively, 11ds, 9ds, and 7ds. Lastly, make a chain of 6ds.

7. On the opposite side of the knot, repeat using floss 3 and 4.

A headband's tapered end displays groups of four rings connected by the same picot.

**Steps: Adding a knot end to the headband's finish**

1. Use a square knot to secure the ends of floss 2 and 3 to one end of the headband. Pull out your #3 needle and attach the two ends by threading them together.

2. When using floss 1 and floss 4 as ball thread, rotate the needle 180 degrees between each color as you alternate 1ds of each. Avoid wrapping the thread around the needle between stitches. Roll the needle back and forth, not continuously in circles. You want the bumpy part of the floss in the stitch in the number 1 to be across from the bumpy part in the floss in the number 4. The objective is a flat band that doesn't curve since it has an equal amount of stitches on either side of the needle, which is a little challenging to master.

With a raised ridge of floss 1 on one side and a raised ridge of floss 4 on the other, it will have a zigzag pattern.

3. Keep working this alternate stitch until you run out of either floss 1 or 4, gradually sliding the stitches off the needle (and onto threads 2 and 3 as needed) as you go. The remaining stitches should be pulled snug but not too tightly. Holding all four threads together, tie an overhand knot in them. Cut the ends off.

4. Carry out step 4 on the opposite side of the headband.

Red is the first floss, green is the fourth, in this close-up of tie-end stitches.

Tie the scarf around your head, with the initial knots positioned in the upper-middle. Wear as a headband. Because the embroidery floss is so smooth, one drawback is that you might need to use bobby pins to hold it in place.

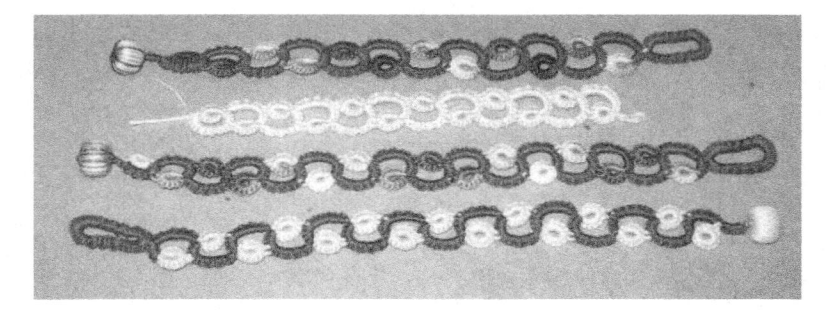

If you read this post all the way through, you have all you need to start tatting most patterns. Please let me know in the comments if

anything is unclear, and I'll try my best to clear it up.

## CHAPTER THREE RINGS JOINED BY NEEDLE TATTING

learning how to join a ring that has been tatted with a needle:

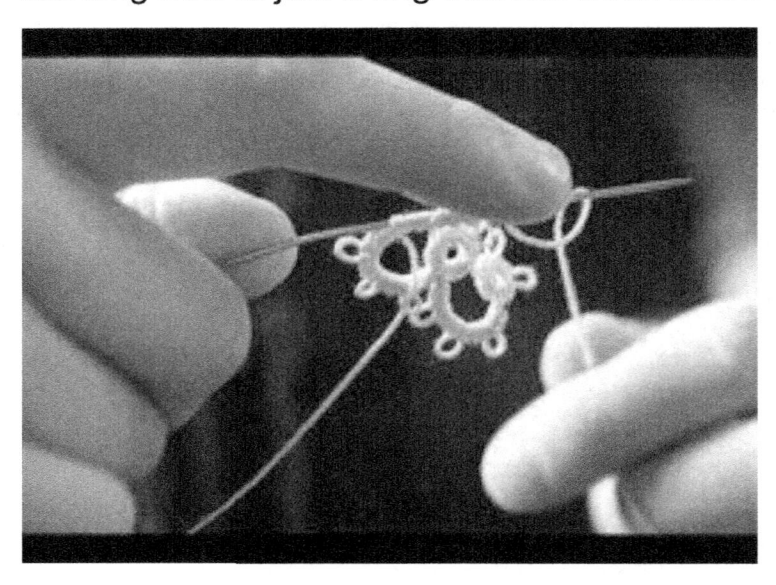

1. When creating lace, newly tatted parts are joined to previously tatted elements. Make a standard practice ring with picots for this exercise using a cut piece of thread.

Pattern: Close ring, 3 ds picot, 3 ds picot, 3 ds picot.

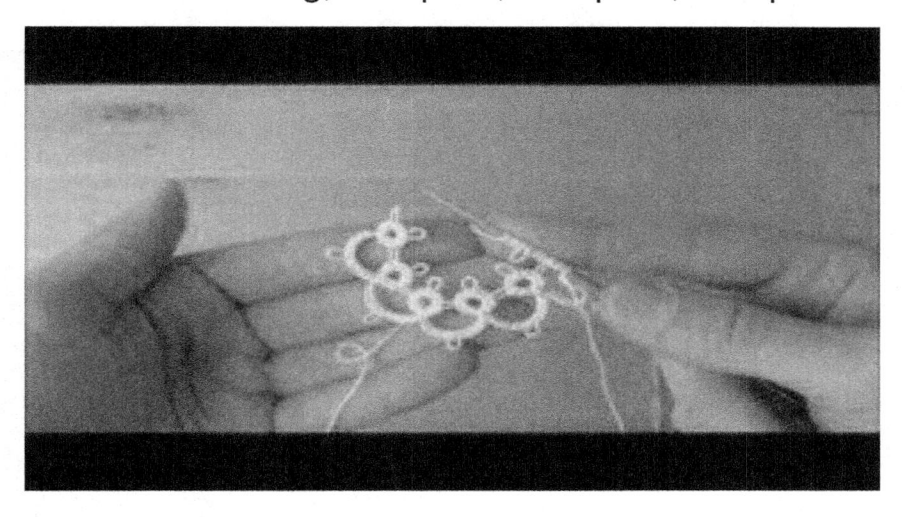

2. Once all the ds have been wrapped, put them over the needle's eye and close them into a genuine ring.

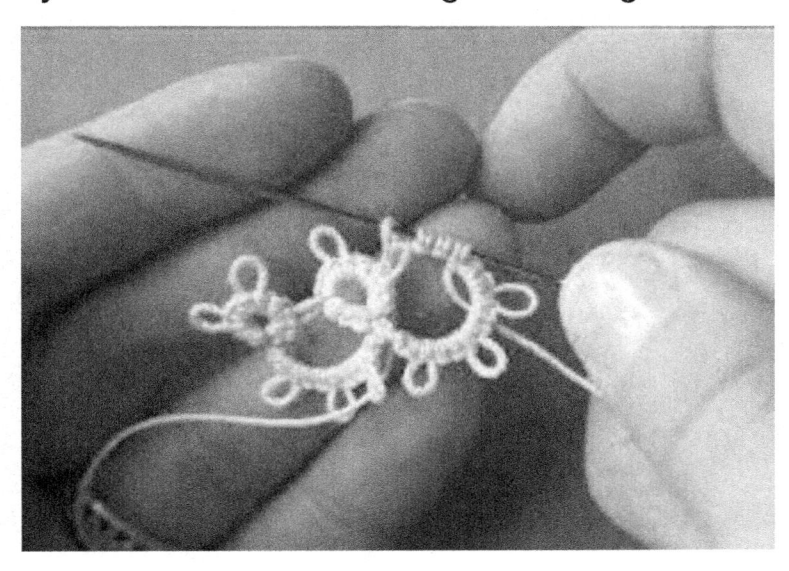

3. Take a close look at the ring. You are facing the front side. Be aware that the picot's legs are divided by bars. The bars denote the work's front.

4. Check out the ring's reverse. The absence of bars from the pico's legs denotes the work's reverse side.

5. Let's now connect one tatted piece to another tatted element. The simplest approach is to simply wrap ds after passing the needle through a picot.

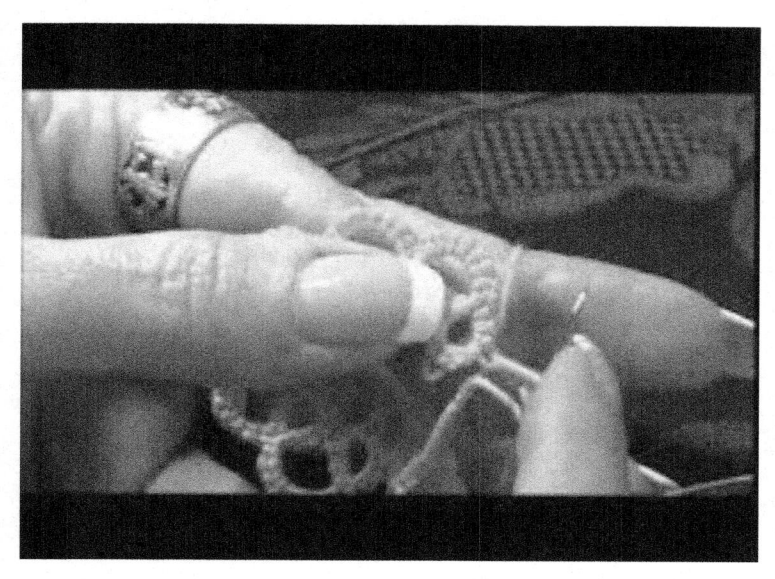

6. Placing the wrapping thread UNDER a picot and using the point of the needle to pull UP a loop and slide it onto the needle is a neater method of joining.

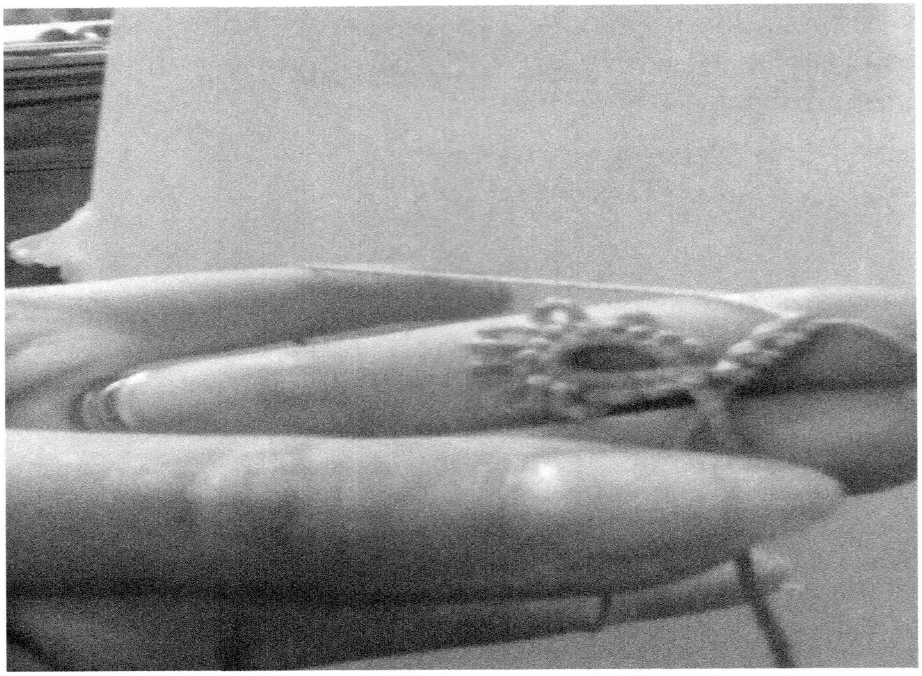

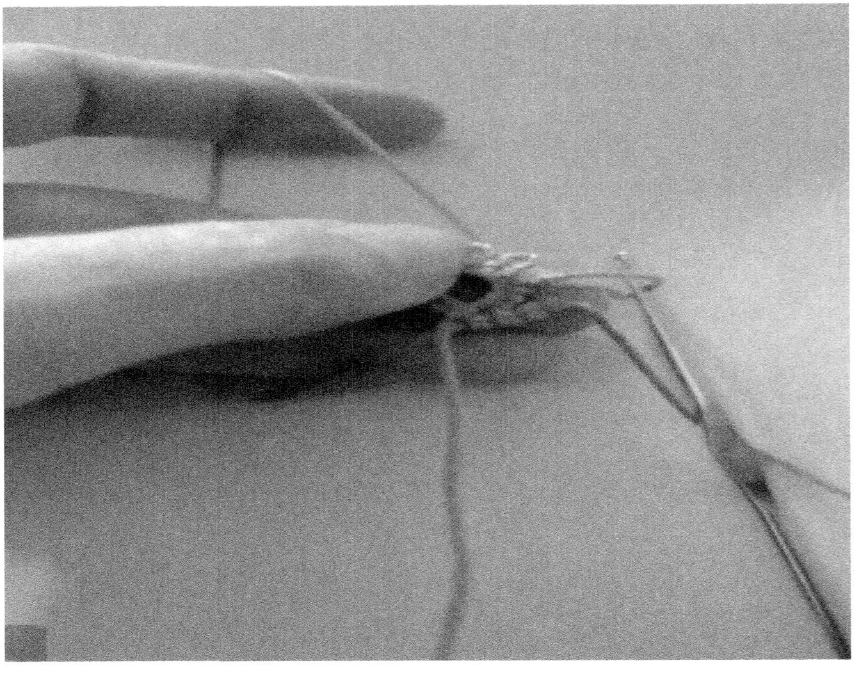

37

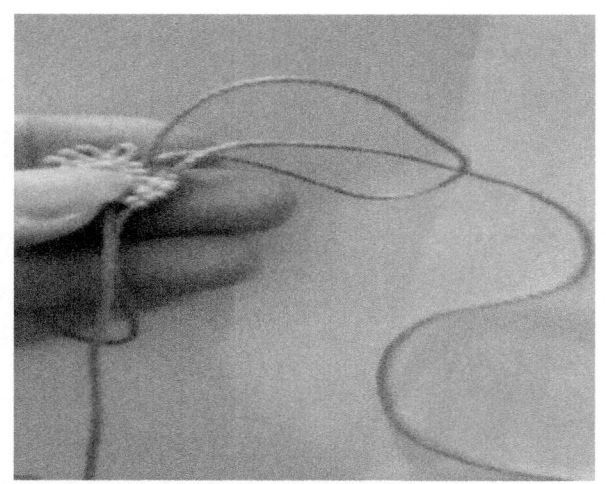

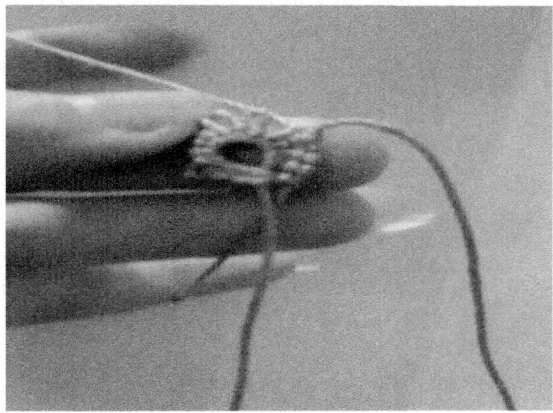

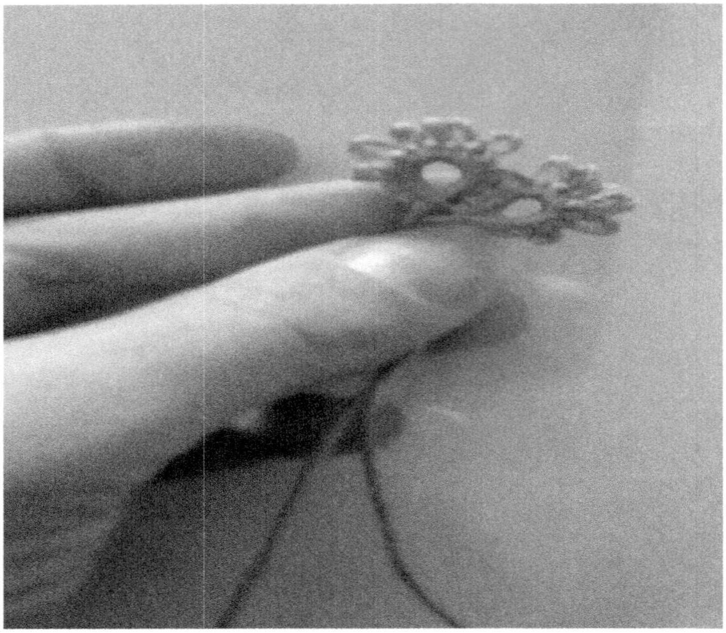

To take up any remaining slack and continue wrapping ds, pull downward on the wrapping thread. Take a look at the picot's joining legs. The new rings lack bars, whereas the original picot had bars. The conventional way of joining is with this UP join.

7. Today, there is an alternate technique that improves the appearance of the finished tatting. Put the wrapping thread on TOP of the picot and draw DOWN a loop of thread using the needle's point. To remove the slack and continue wrapping, slide the loop over the needle and tug on the wrapping thread. s 8. Recheck the picot's legs. Now, on both rings, you can see bars spanning the picot legs. It is known as the DOWN join.

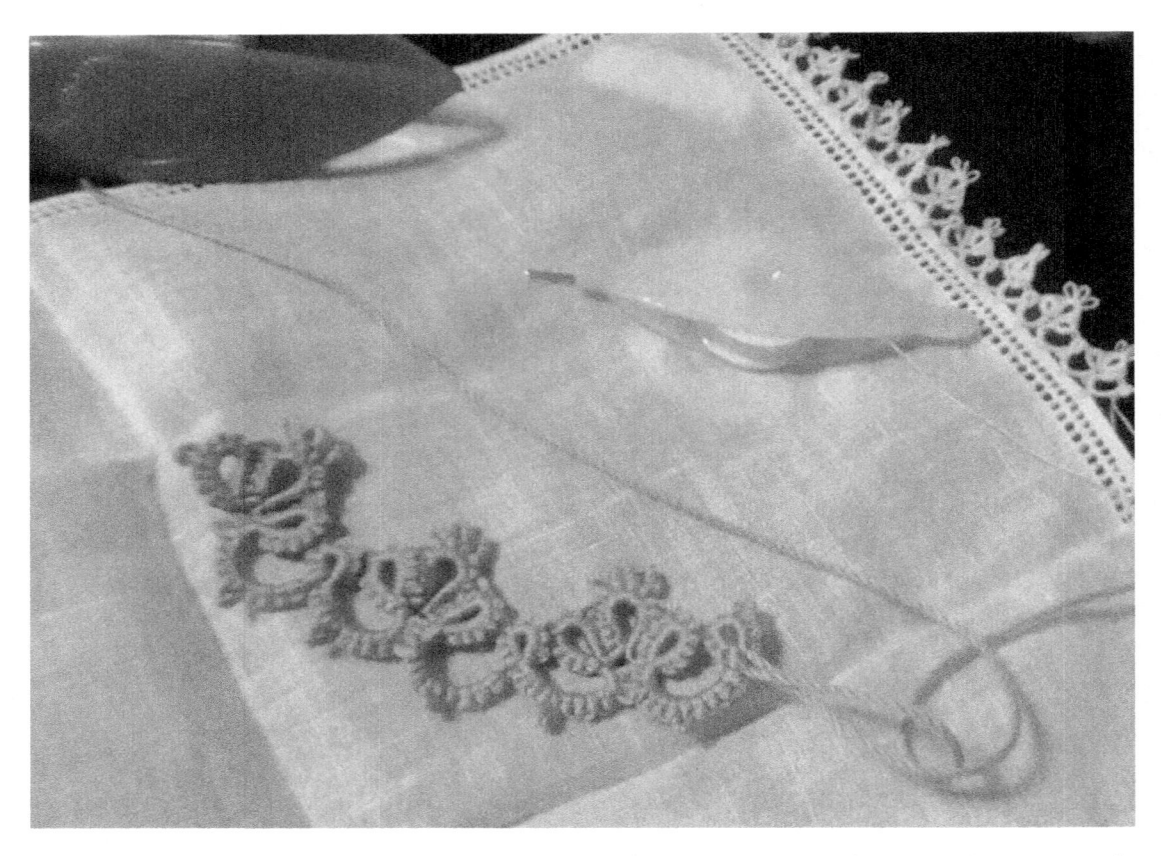

Use the same join across the project once you've chosen the sort of join you want to employ. Have fun tatting.

**CHAPER FOUR**

# HOW TO TAT: HOW TO MAKE RINGS AND PICOTS

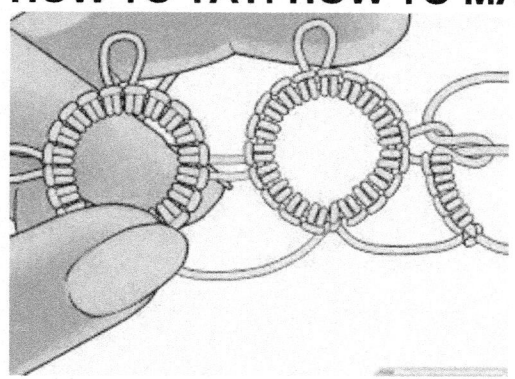

There are rings and picots in every tatting pattern. The ring serves as the design's starting point. The picots are used for joining as well as for ornamentation. To make the stages apparent in your mind, these instructions are given in full. You'll be able to read the instructions exactly as they would appear in a tatting pattern once you've mastered this. To help the newbie, this tutorial offers tatting words' acronyms.

**First Ring, Method 1.**

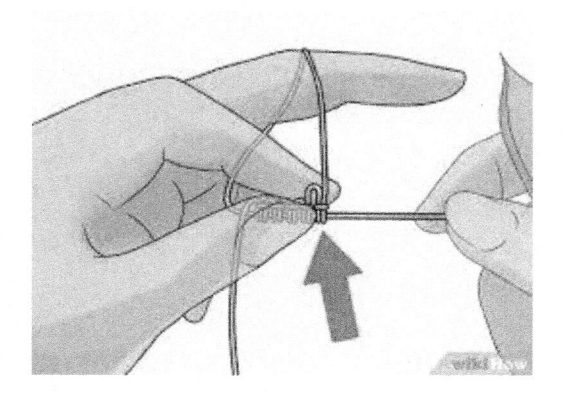

1 Keep in mind that the working stitch will always fall between the thumb and the first finger. Figures 12, 13, and 14 call for the fingers to come from the location indicated by the arrow. To ensure that all

the stages are apparent, the drawings are created in this way (keeping the fingers away from the working stitch).

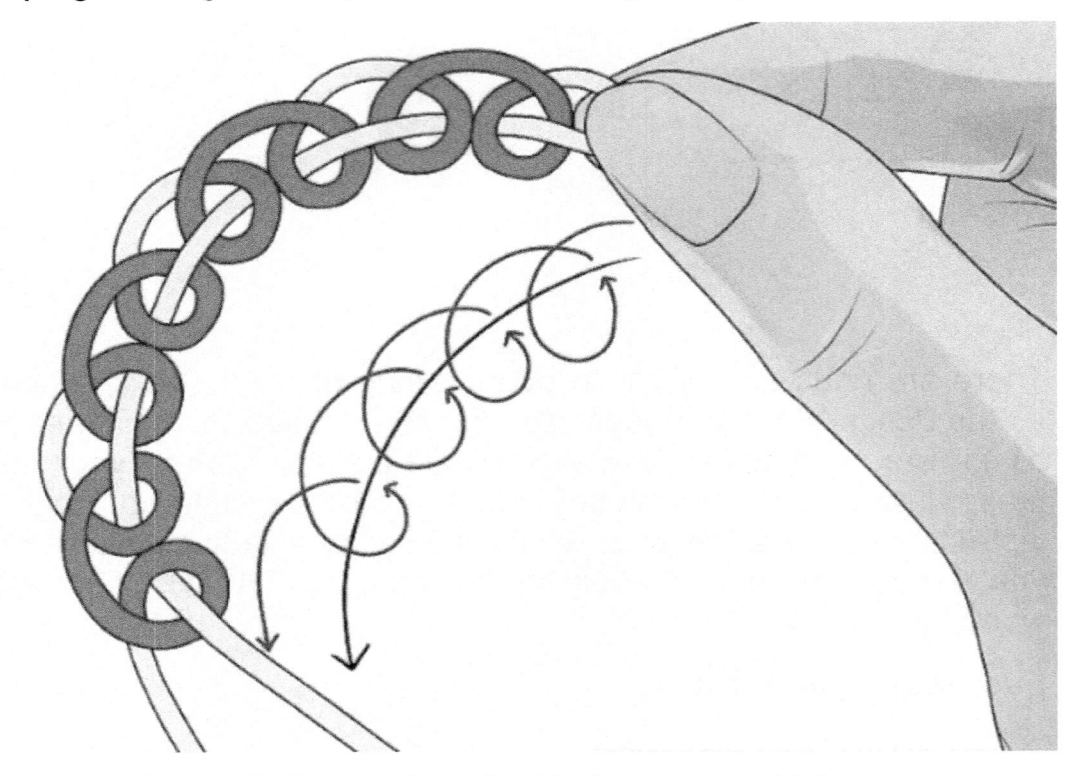

2 .Ring the first bell. Create four double hemmings (ds).

¼ in

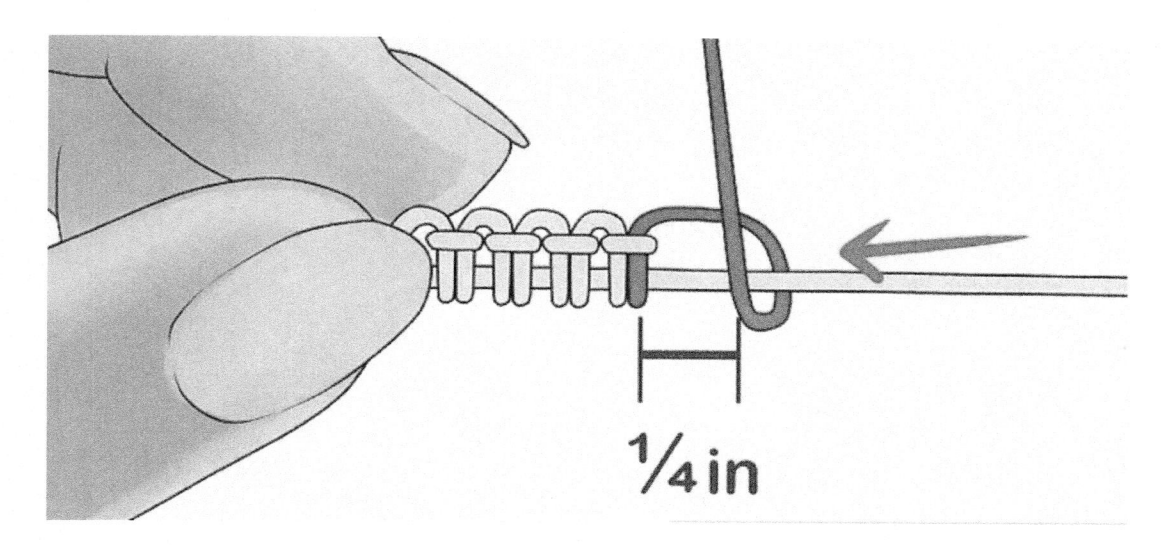

3.

Make the first half of a double stitch in step three (ds). But when you move it into place, stop about 14 inch (0.6 cm) from the double stitch before that (ds).

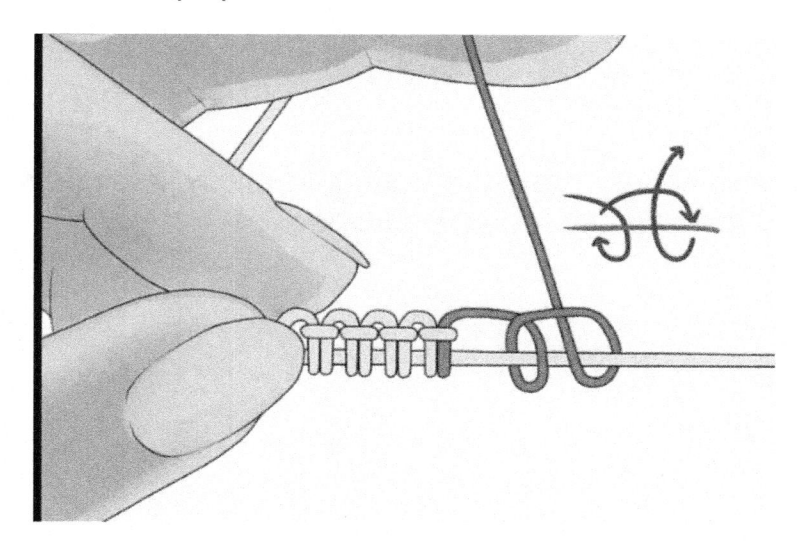

4.

Finish off the double stitch (ds).

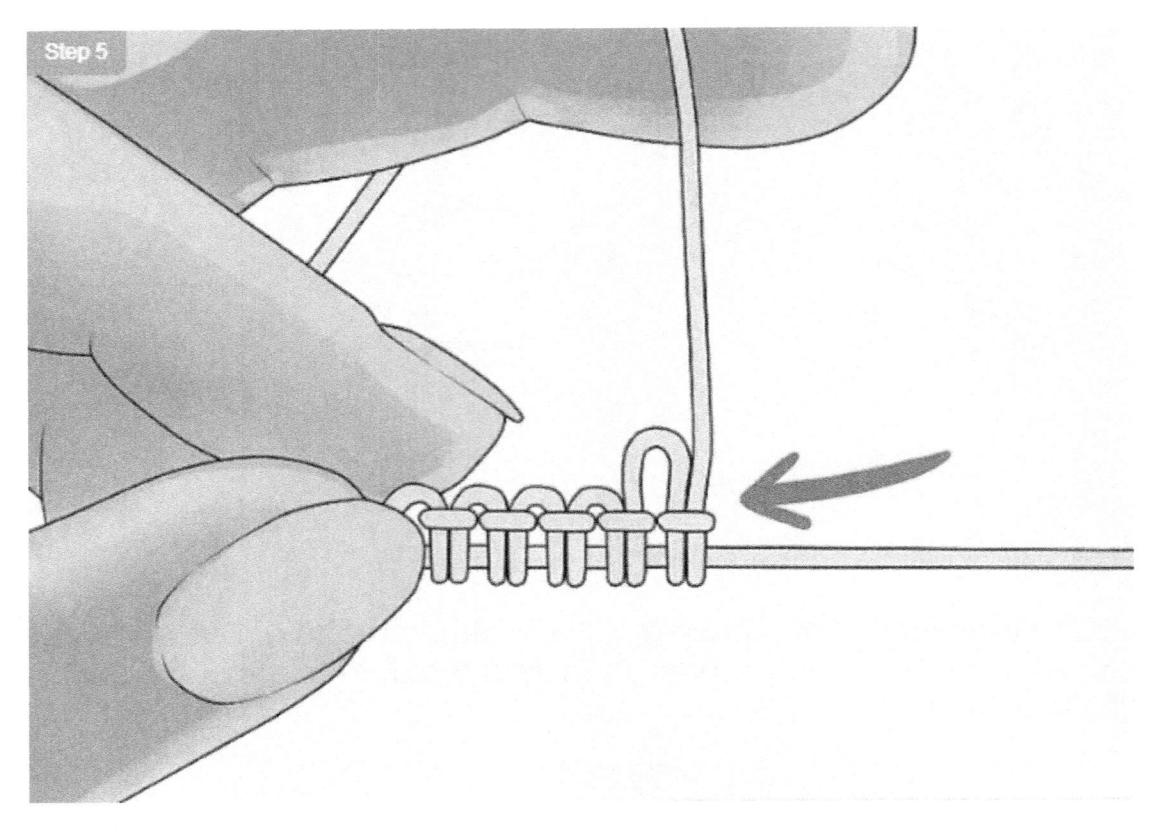

5.

Close to the first four stitches, draw the complete stitch. A picot is a little loop created by the gap between the stitches (p).

6.

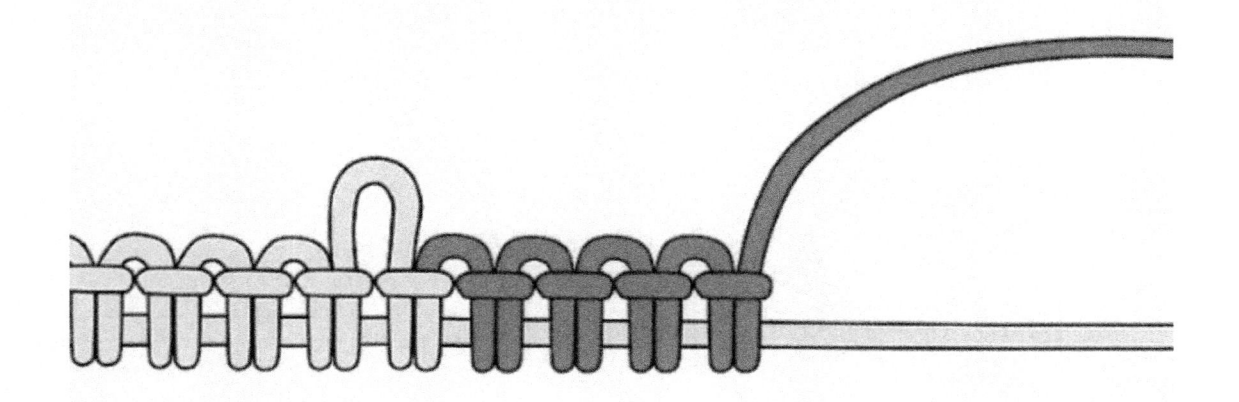

4 more double stitches, totaling 6. (ds).

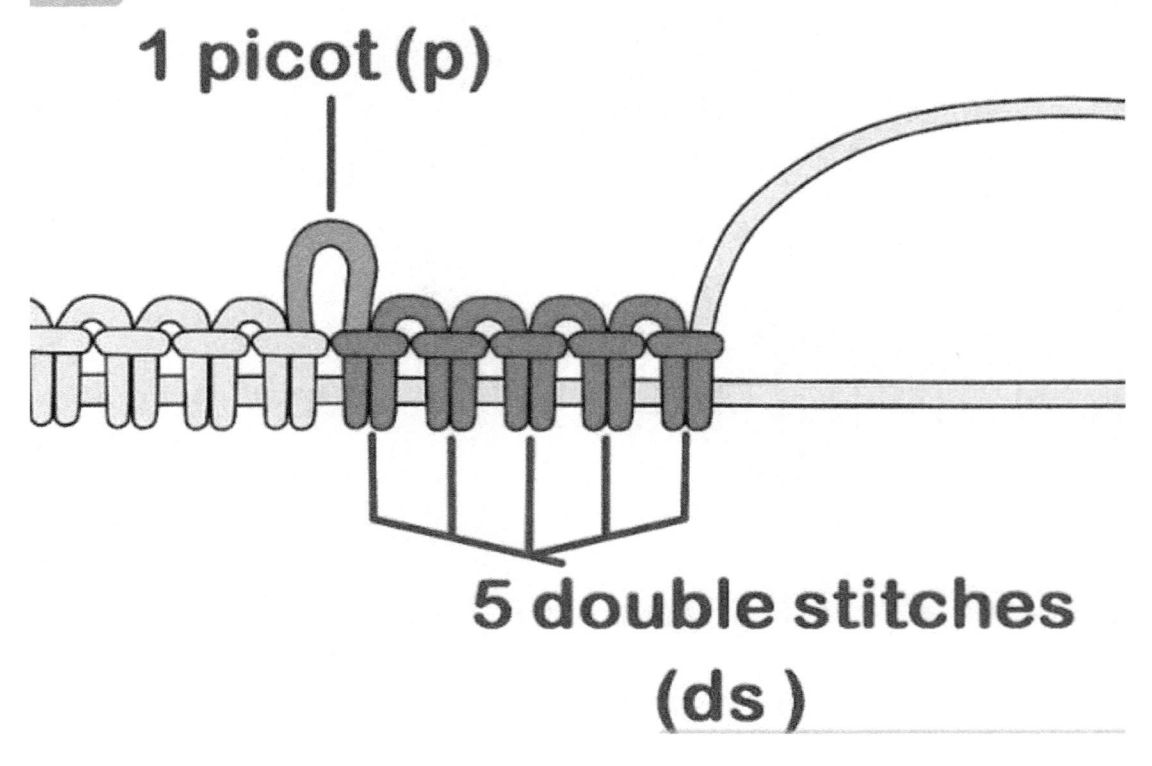

7.

Take note that the creation is described as "1 picot (p) and 5 double stitches (ds)". A picot simply refers to the loop; it excludes the double stitch that secures the loop.

Step 8

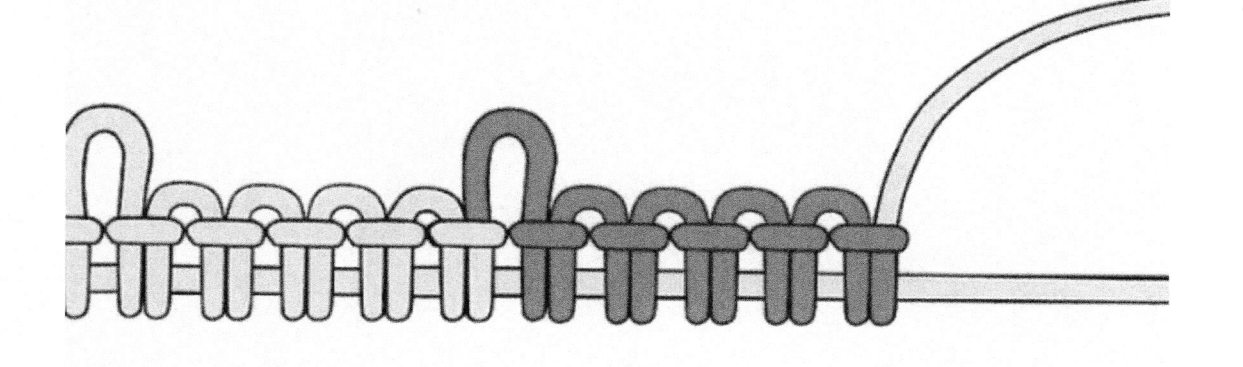

8.

Add five double stitches and one more picot (see previous step).

9.

Step 9

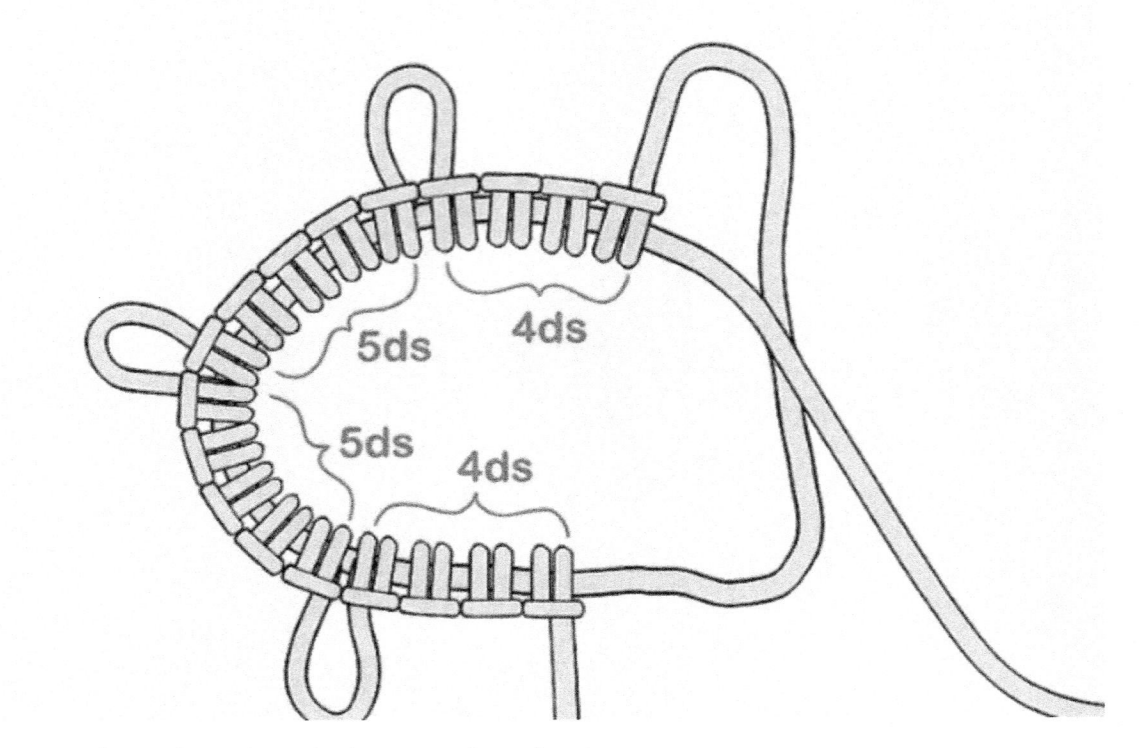

Work four double stitches and a picot.

10.

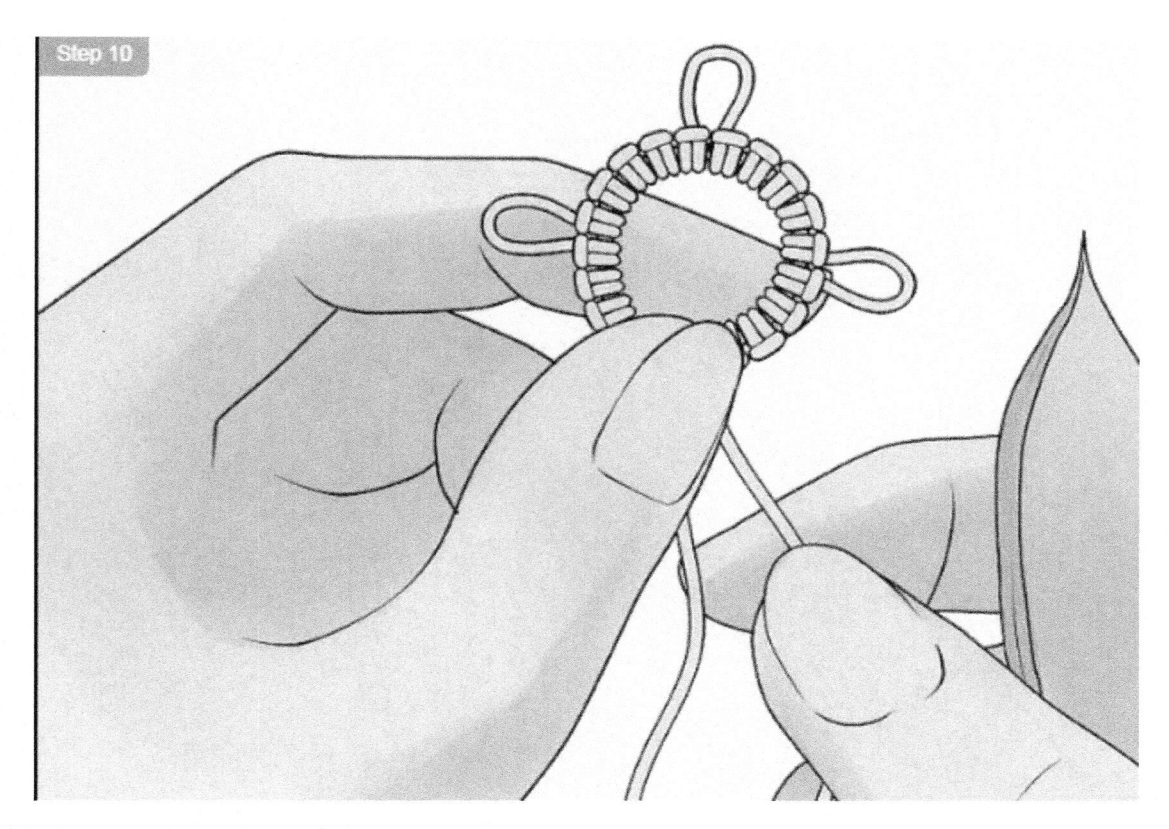

Between the left hand's thumb and forefinger, firmly grasp the sutures. The first and last stitches should meet to form a ring when you tighten the shuttle thread.

**Second Ring and Joining 1 in Method 2**

Step 1

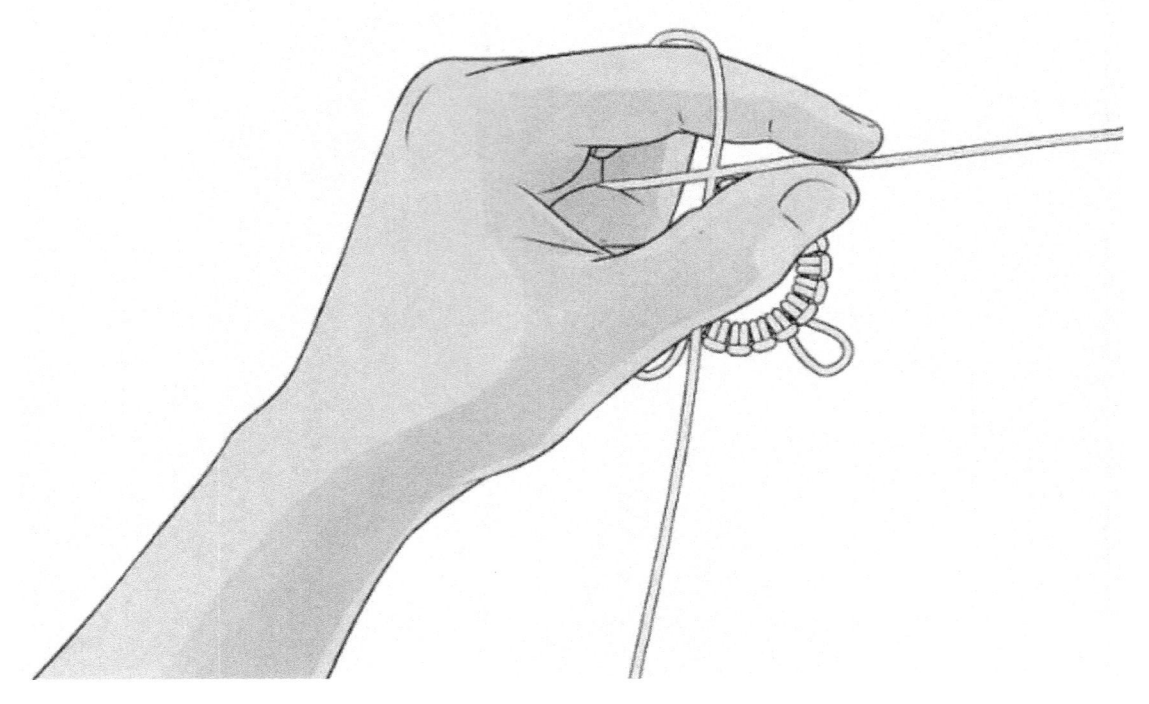

1 To prepare for a second ring, wind the thread around your left hand.

2.

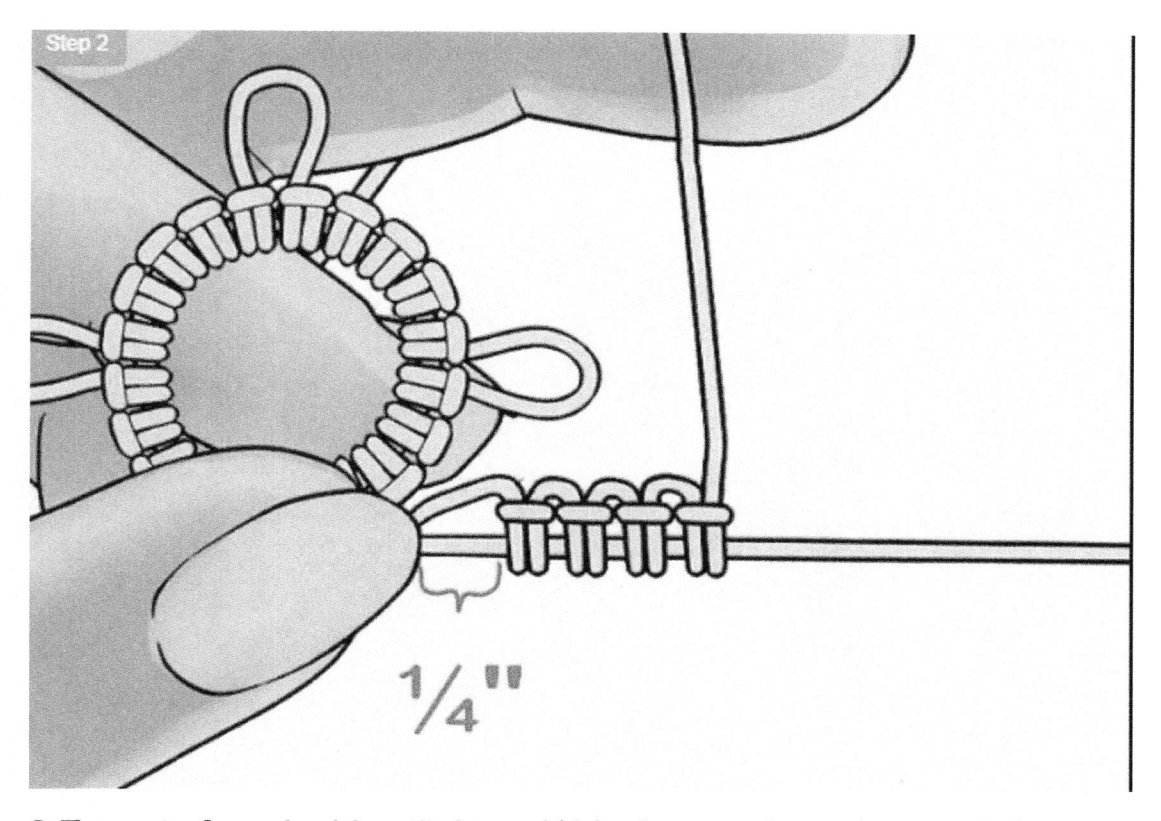

2 Execute four double stitches. 1/4 inch away from the newly formed ring.

3.

Step 3

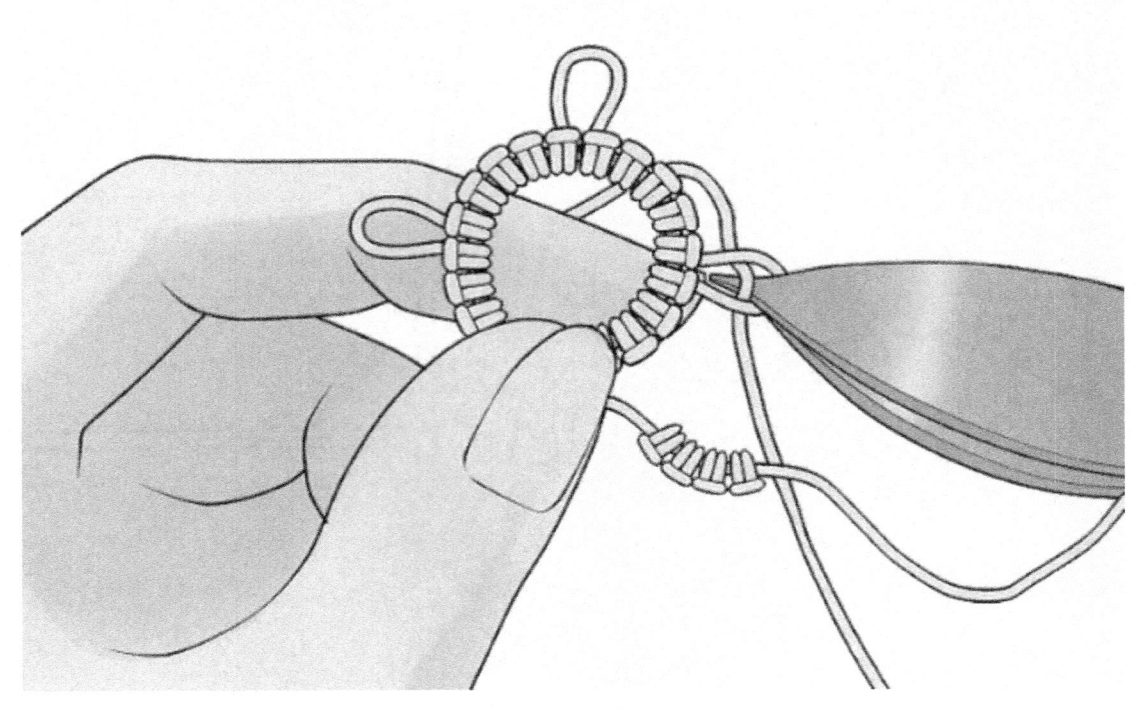

3 To catch the thread surrounding the left hand, insert the shuttle's pointed end through the final picot of the previous ring.

4.

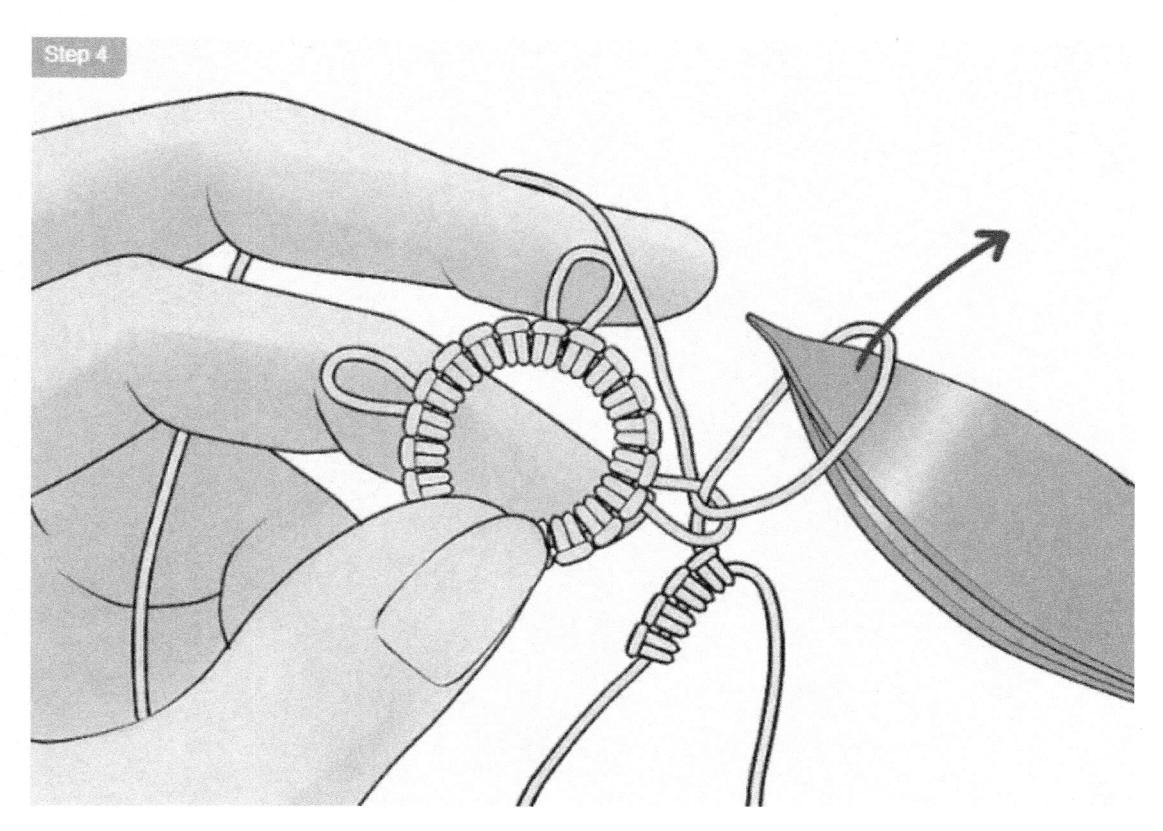

4

Till there is a loop big enough to fit the shuttle, pull the thread through.

5.

Step 5

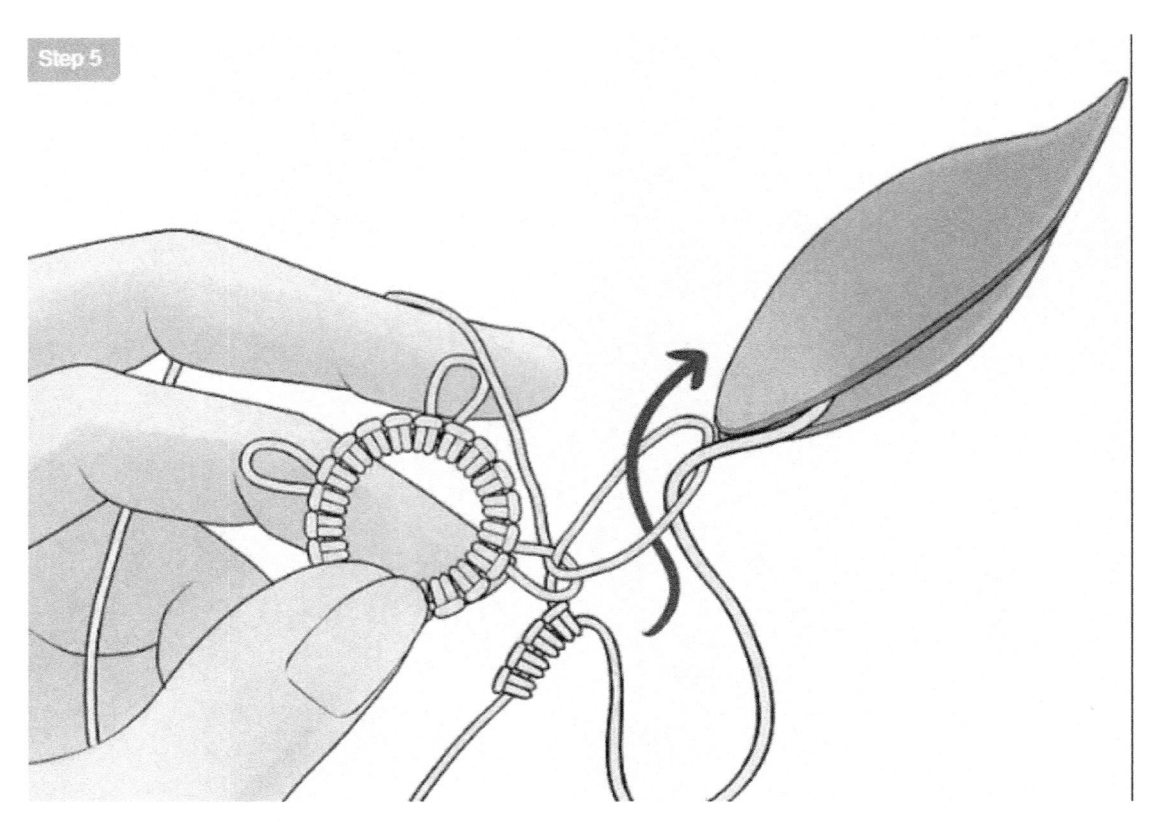

5 Draw the shuttle thread tight by pulling the shuttle through the loop.

6.

Step 6

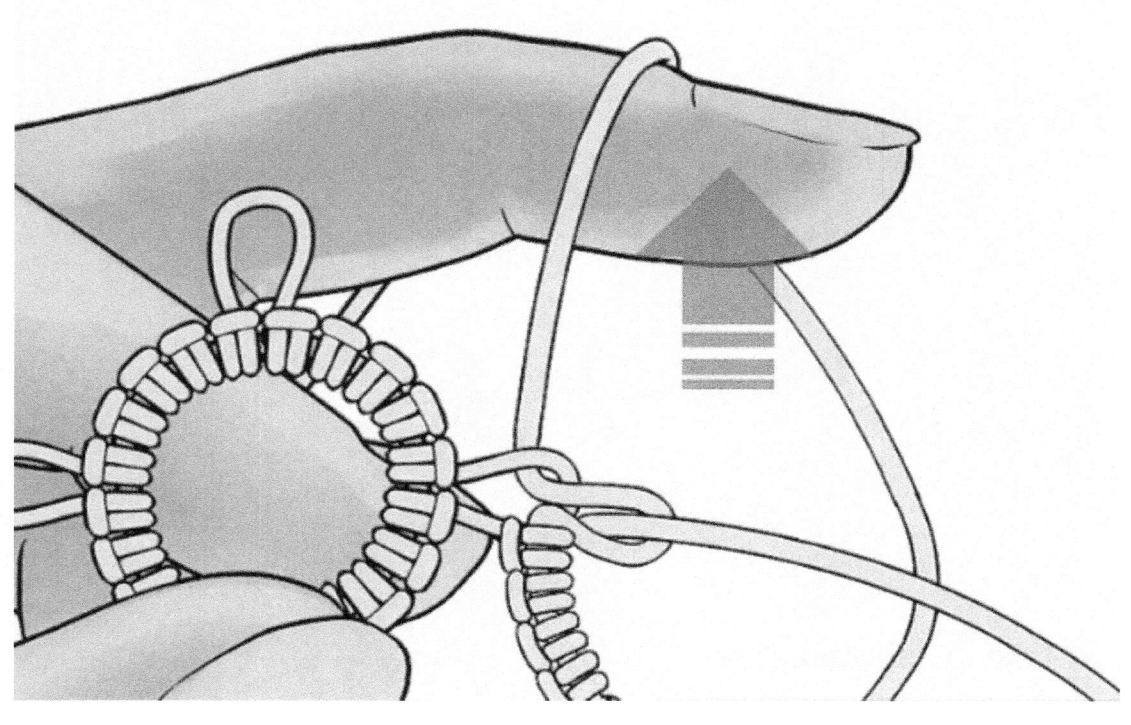

6

To draw up the loop, slowly lift the middle finger of your left hand. This completes the previous double stitch and attaches the new ring to the previous one.

7.

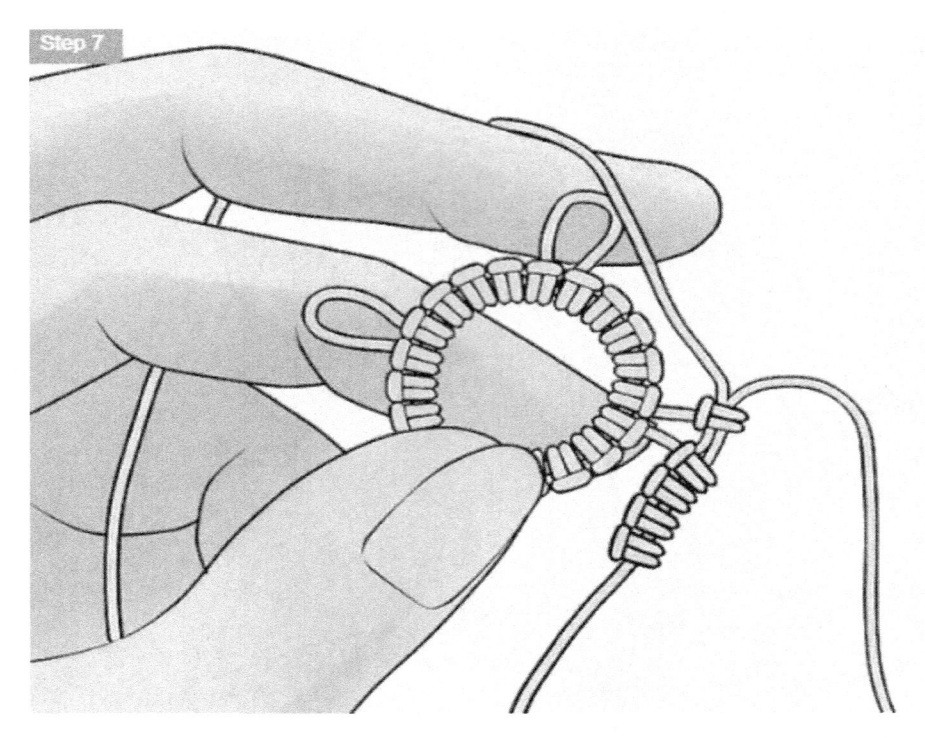

7 Make the second stitch.

8.

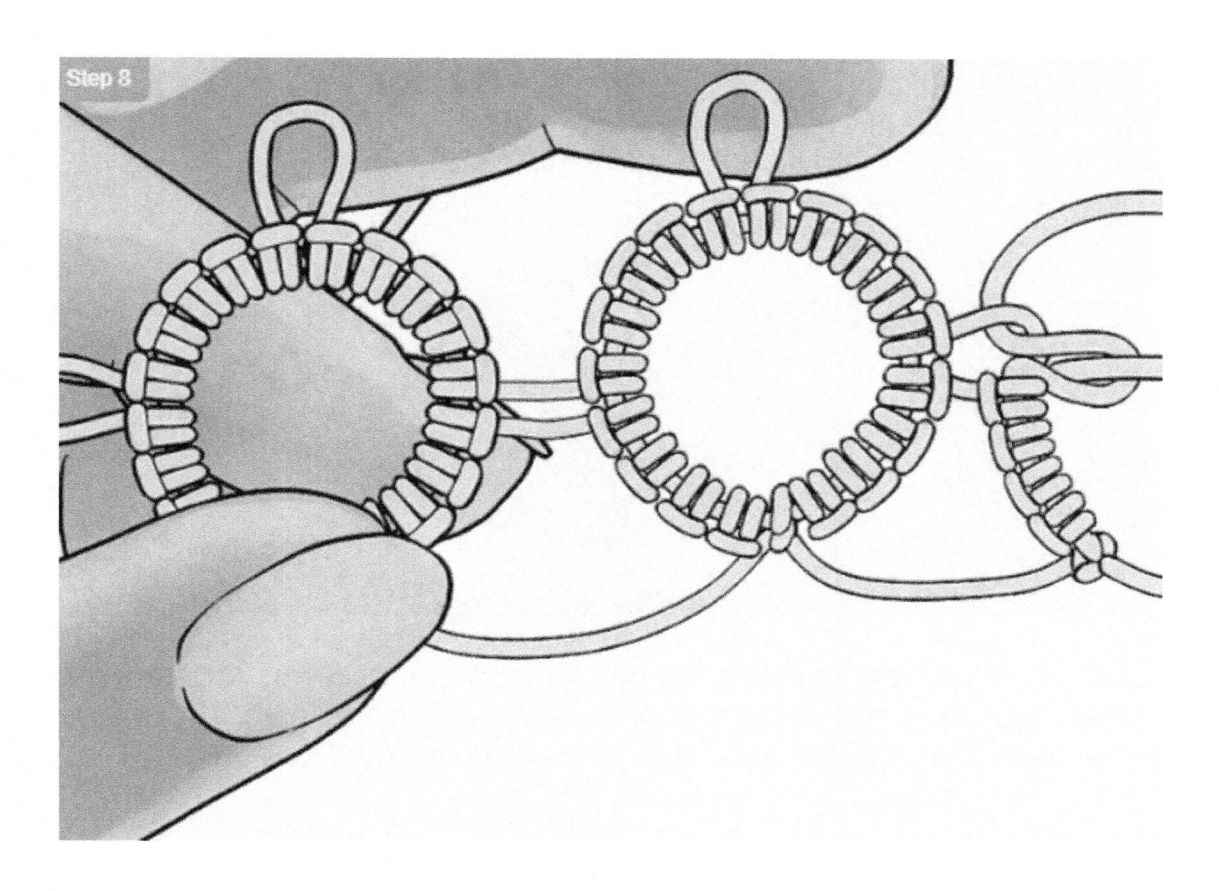

## CHAPER FIVE

### INTRODUCTION: A BEGINNER PROJECT: TATTED SNOWFLAKE ORNAMENTS

This tatting project is designed for beginners. Once you've produced a couple, you can learn how to modify a design to give it a unique spin. After that, it's rather simple to create your own designs.

You might find the process to be slow at first, which is why I made these little. You will be able to work these up pretty rapidly once your skills improve. Go ahead and attempt a larger project at that moment. If your first endeavor is overly ambitious (large and difficult), you will become discouraged and give up.

This technique for producing lace dates back at least to Elizabethan times. I saw a painting of a very elegant-looking woman dressed in Elizabethan attire posing for her portrait while obviously bored to tears. She tatted while the time passed. The lace-work maker's as well as the exquisitely carved shuttle she was using were painted by the artist. By learning to tat, you can contribute to the preservation of a stunning art form for at least one more generation.

**Initial Step: Materials**

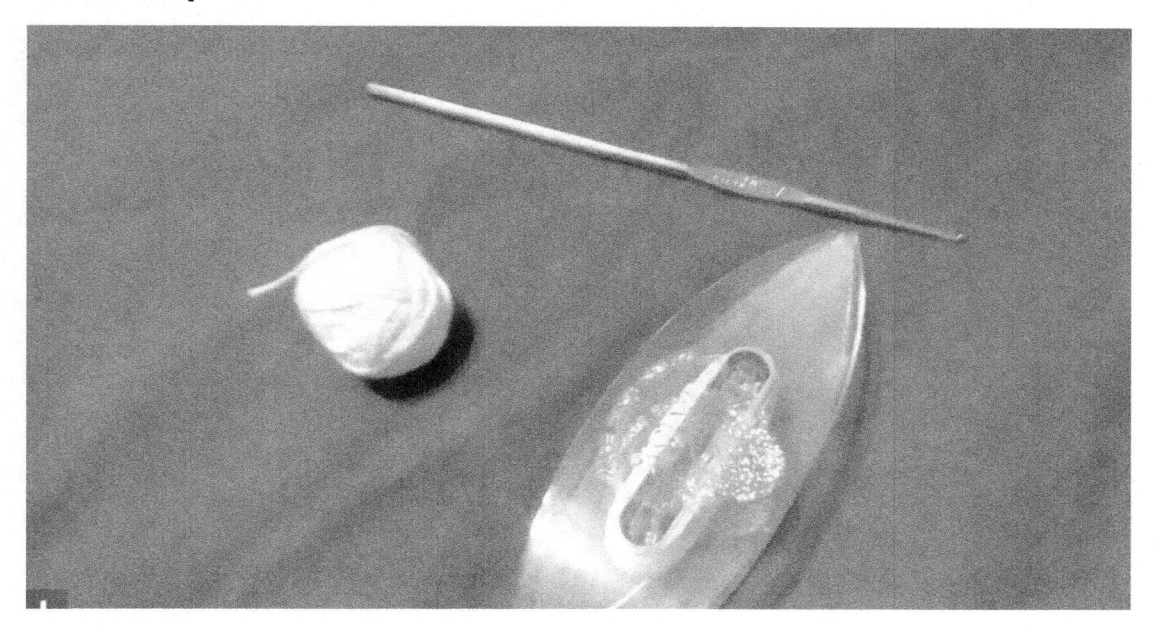

Thread: Hand quilting thread or thinner crochet cotton for little ornaments, thicker crochet cotton for large ornaments.

Shuttle and hook—these may be produced as distinct items or as a single tool.

Stiffening the ornament with white glue or spray starch is optional.

Every pattern's instructions:

Double hitch is denoted by "dh," and picot by "p."

**Step 2: First ornament**

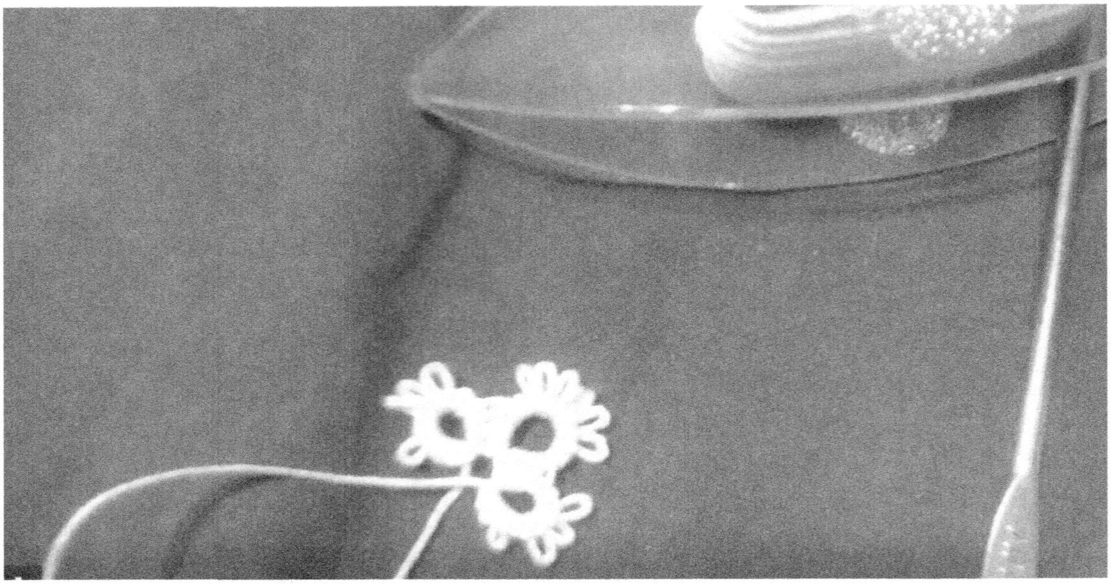

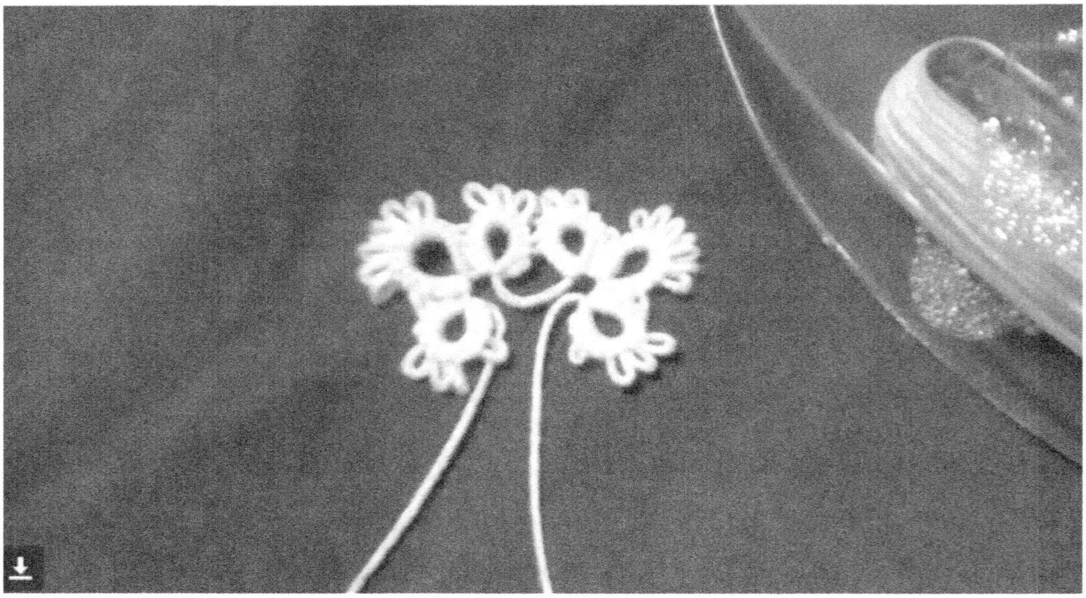

There are no chains in this one; simply rings.

Put thread in the shuttle.

Ring #1: 4 dh, p, 3 p, 1 dh, p, 1 dh, p, 3 p, 4 dh, close ring

Ring #2: 4 dh, link to the final p of the previous ring, 2 dh, p, 1 dh, p, 1 dh, p, 2 dh, p, 4 dh, close ring.

Ring #3: 4 dh; link to final p of preceding ring; 3 dh; p; 1 dh; p; 1 dh; p; 3 dh; p; 4 dh; close ring.

A group of rings is formed by these 3 rings. I had 6 of these clusters planned. Since I was using up thread that was already in my shuttle and there wasn't enough for more than five clusters, I was only able to complete five clusters.

Repeat the cluster, joining to the last p of the previous cluster when you reach the first p of the first ring. To keep the clusters apart from one another, start the first ring of the subsequent cluster about 1/2 inch from the base of the preceding cluster.

Repeat the process six more times (or 5 clusters in my case). In the first cluster, the first p joins the last p of the previous cluster. If needed, stiffen.

**Ornament No. 2 in Step 3**

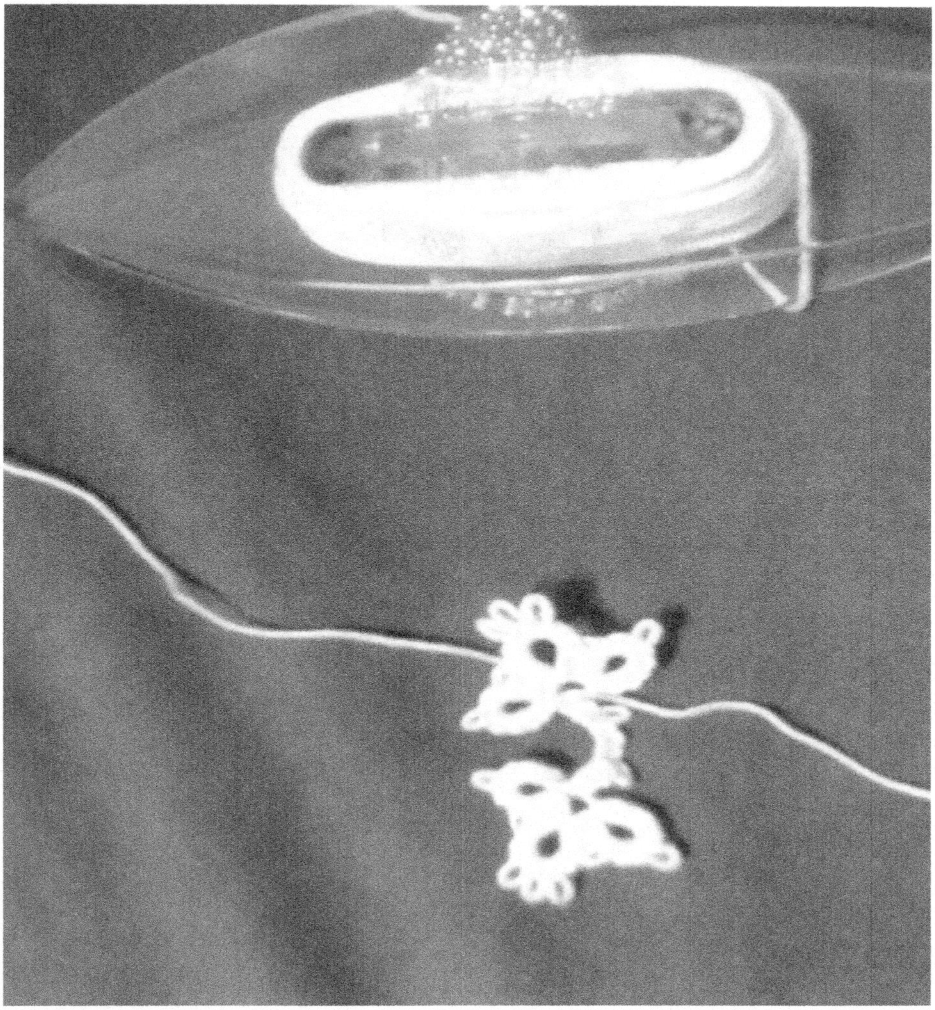

This snowflake is slightly more complex due of the chains that connect the clusters.

A yard of thread should be unwound. About a yard from the end of your thread, begin the first ring. When you tat the chains, you will use this tail.

Ring #1—6 dh, p, 3 dh, p, and close the ring.

Ring #2: 3 dh, p, 1 dh, p, 3 dh, close ring, join to last p of preceding ring.

Ring #3: 3 dh, p, 3 dh, p, 3 dh, close ring, join to last p of preceding ring.

These 3 rings are grouped together.

Use your hand to encircle the tail thread while you tat the chain's dh.

Chain: 3 dh, p, 4 dh, p, 3 dh, tighten.

Make the following cluster.

Form the following chain, except connect the first p to the last p of the preceding chain.

Up till there are 6 clusters, repeat this method. Make one chain after the sixth cluster by joining the first p to the last p of the preceding chain AND the first p of the first chain. Trim the ends of the thread after tying a tight knot with the two ends. If needed, stiffen.

**Fourth step: Ornament #3**

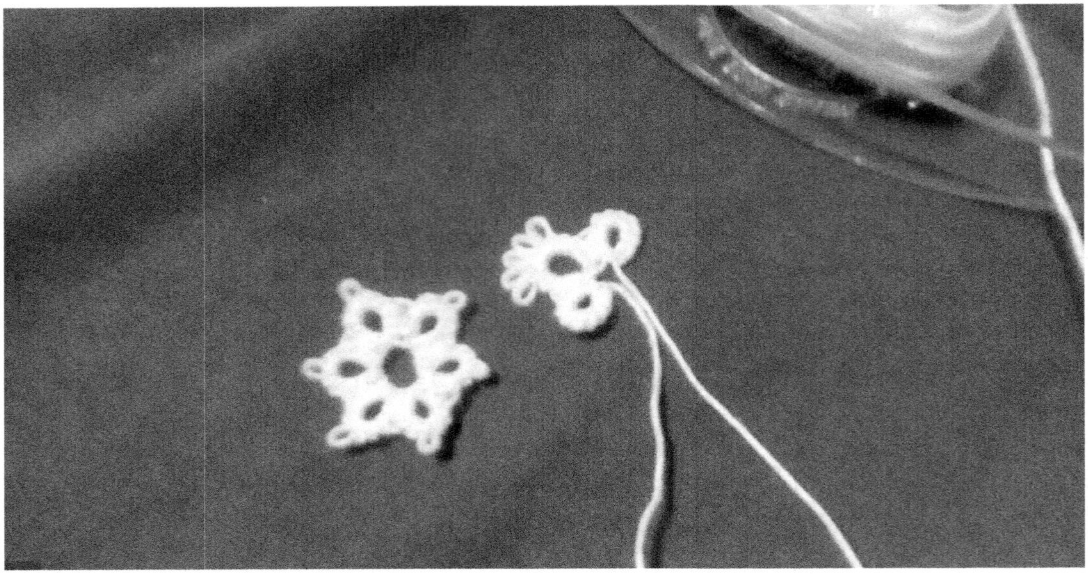

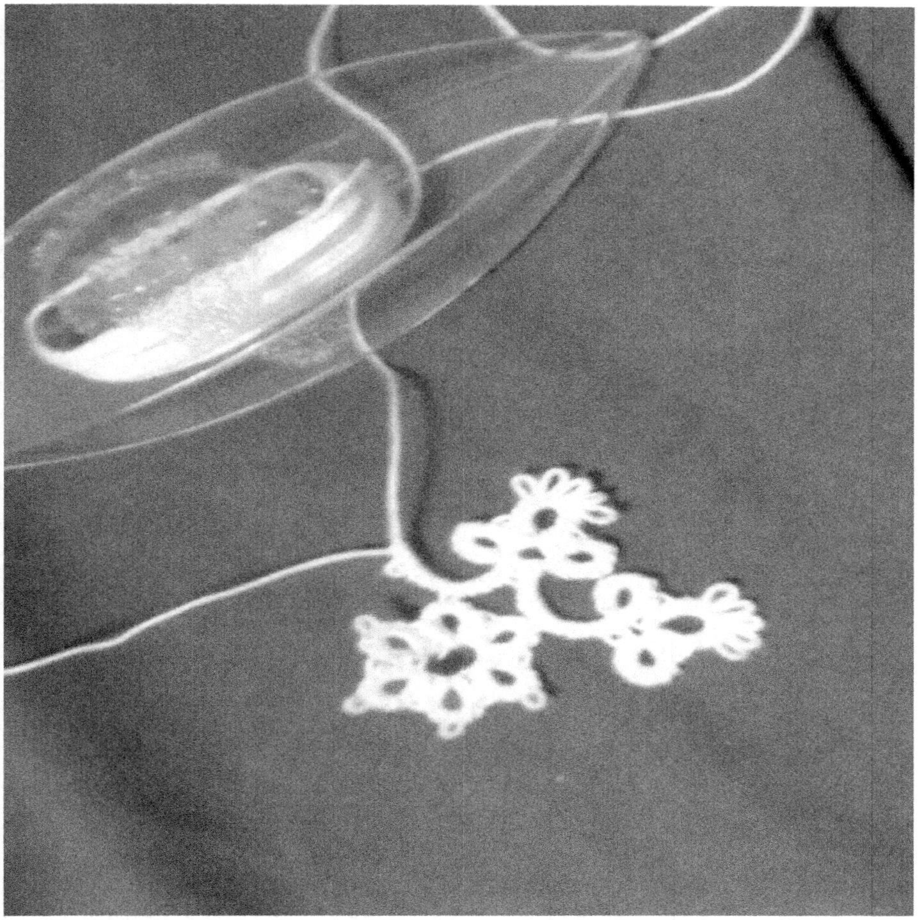

In two rounds, this snowflake was created.

Round 1: Close the ring, 3 dh, p, 3 dh, p, 3 dh.

Close ring: 3 dh, p, 3 dh, p, 3 dh, p, 3 dh. 3 dh, join to final p of preceding ring.

Once you have six rings, repeat. The first p of the sixth ring connects it to the fifth ring, while the last p of the sixth ring connects it to the first ring.

Trim the threads after tying the ends together.

Unwind roughly a yard and a half of thread for round 2.

start the cluster

Ring #1: Close ring, 9 dh, p, and 3 dh.

Ring No. 2: 3 dh, join, 3 dh, p, dh, p, dh, p, 3 dh, p, 3 dh, shut ring.

Ring #3: Three hands, join, nine hands, close ring.

Chain 2 dh, 2 p, 4 dh, link to 1st round's p, 4 dh, 2 p, and draw taut.

Create one more cluster.

The initial p of the new chain must be joined to the last p of the preceding chain.

Connect the first p to the chain before and the last p to the first p on the sixth chain. Pull firmly. Close any gaps. Reduce tails. If needed, stiffen.

**Fifth step: stiffening**

If you use thicker thread, tatting will likely be stiffer than crochet. This action might not be necessary. I occasionally wait until after a few Christmases, when I see that my tatted ornaments have become droopy, to stiffen them.

White glue and water are combined roughly 50/50. Paint the lace with the mixture. Use a paper towel to absorb any excess. Permit to dry.

Spray starch on as an alternative. Use an iron to heat. Turn it over and proceed once more.

# CHAPTER SIX NECKLACE TATTING WITH A NEEDLE

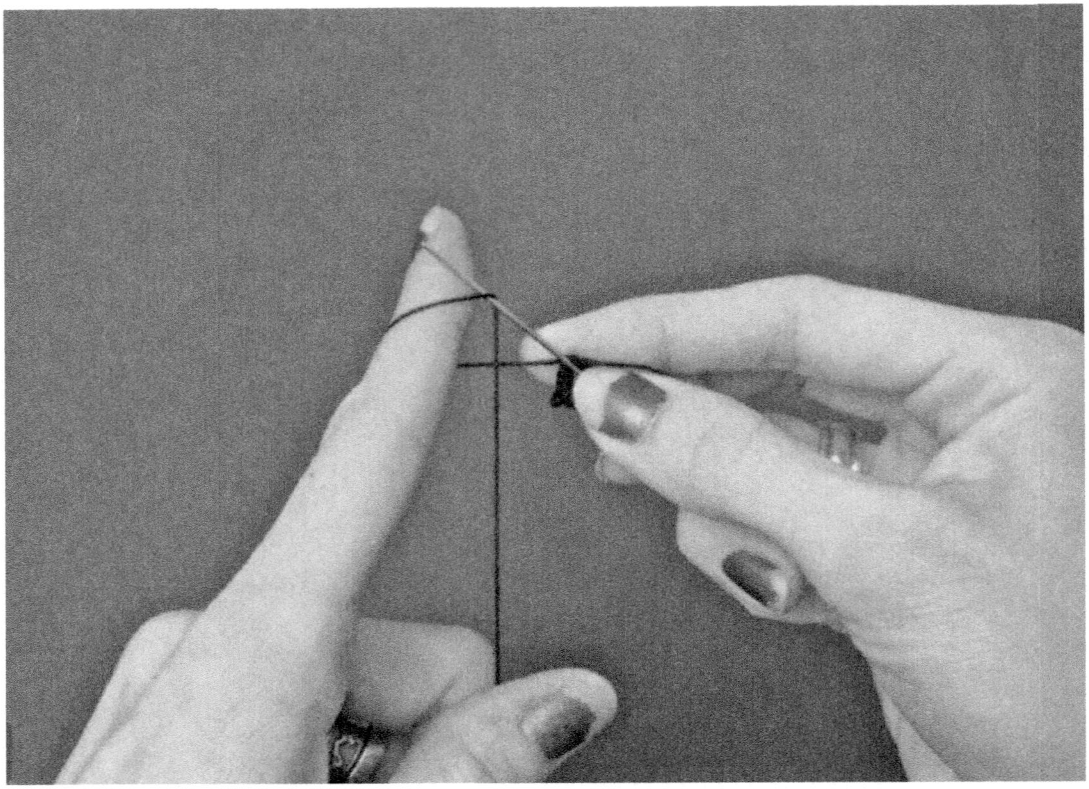

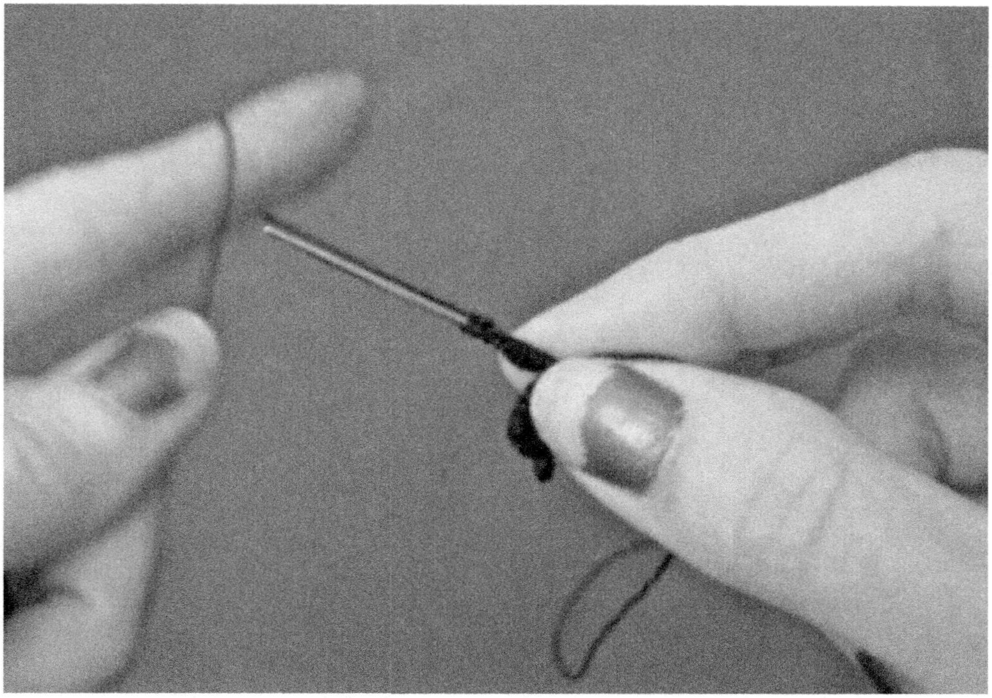

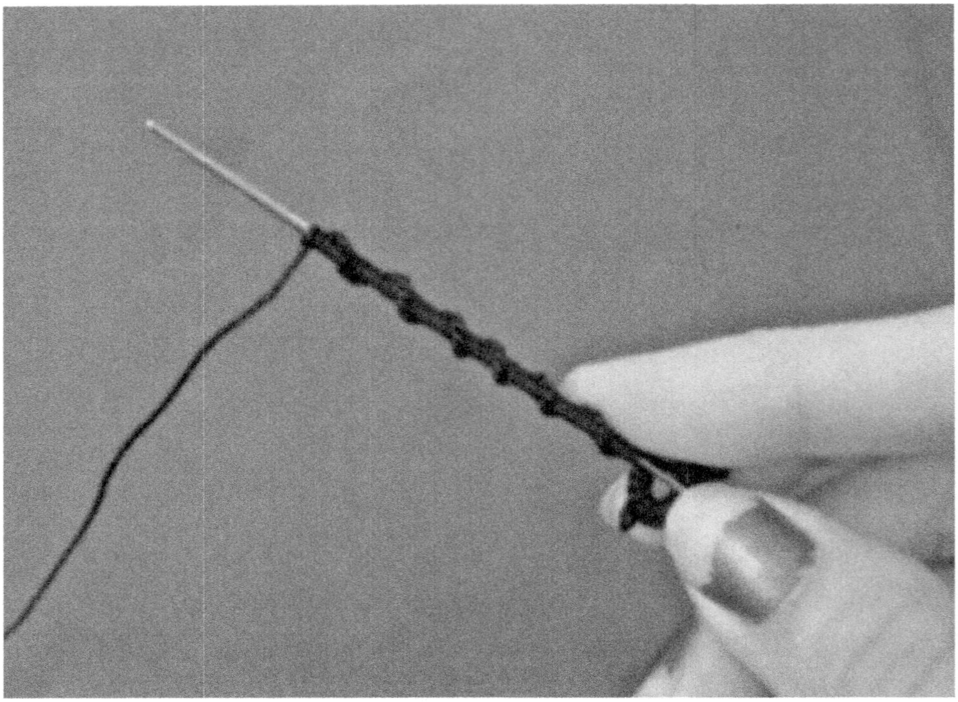

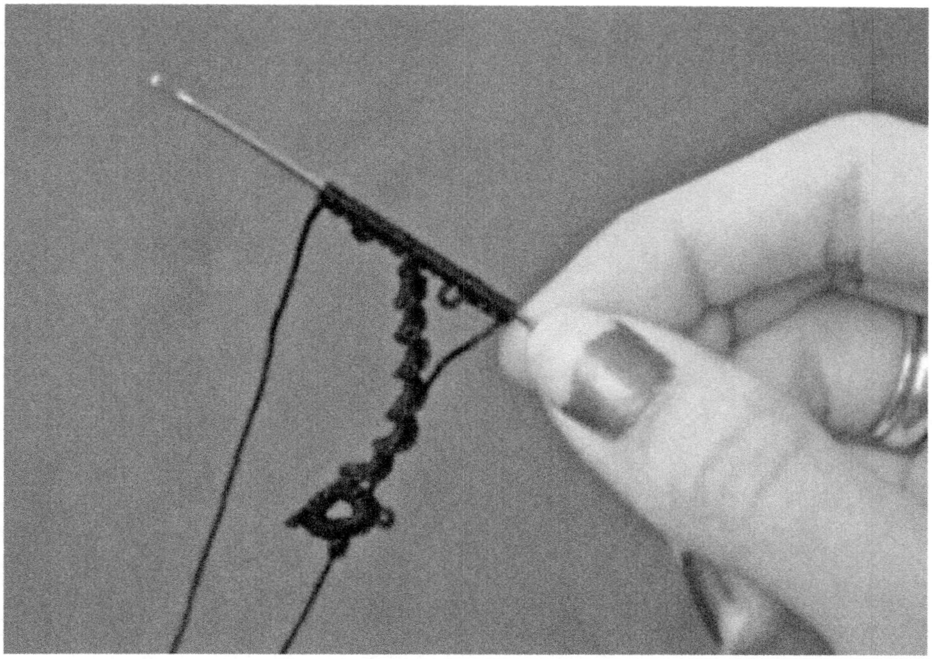

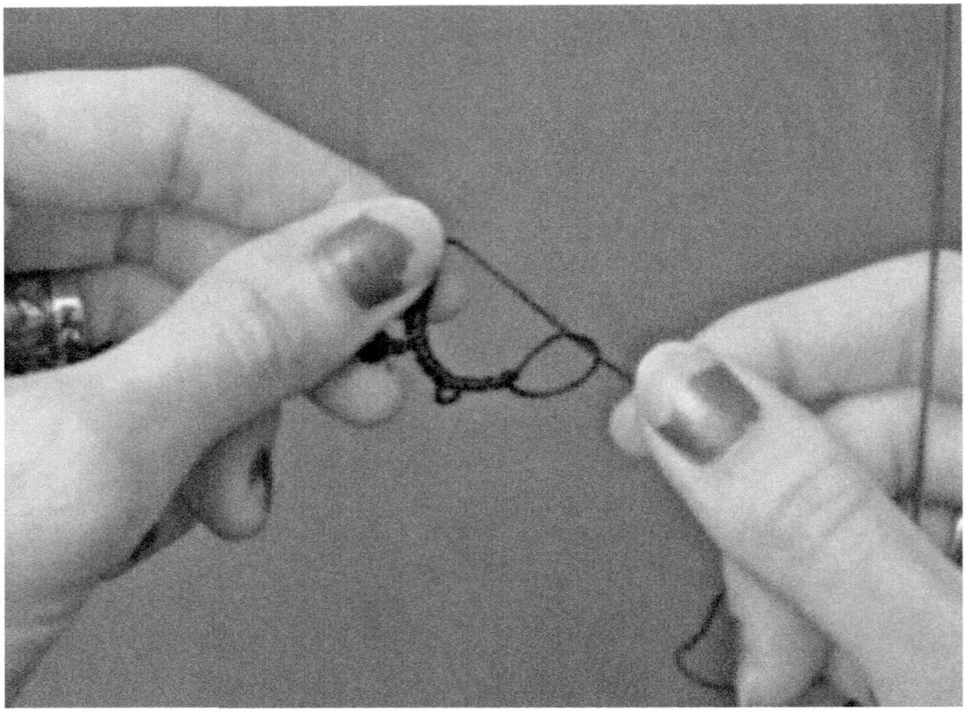

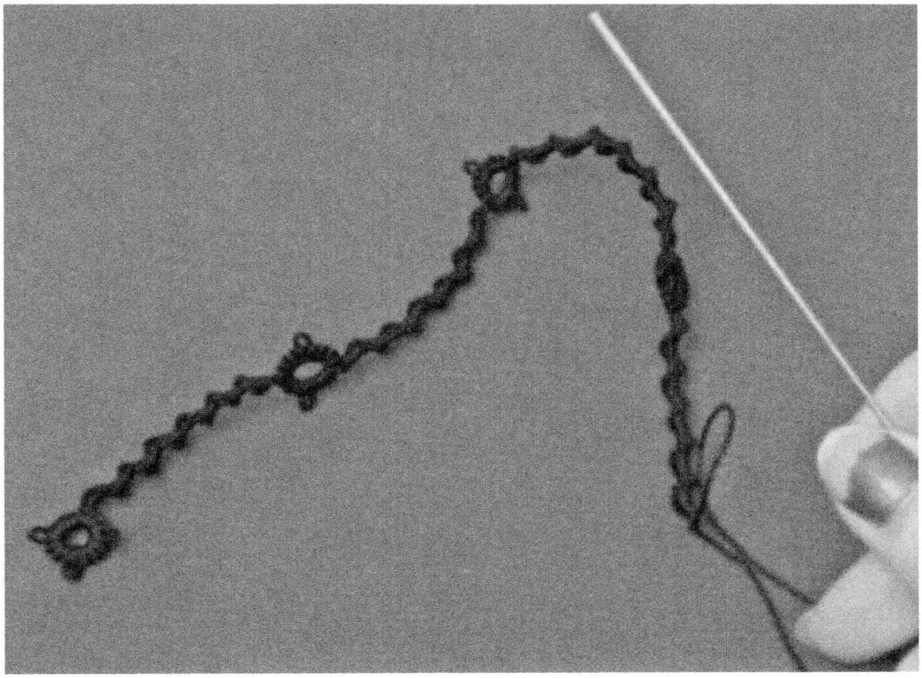

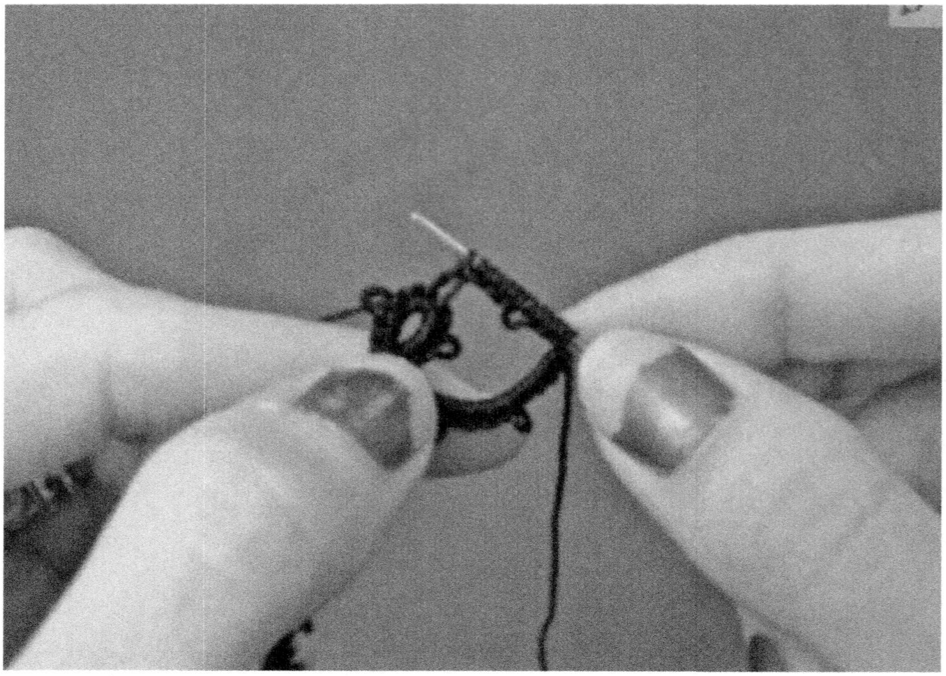

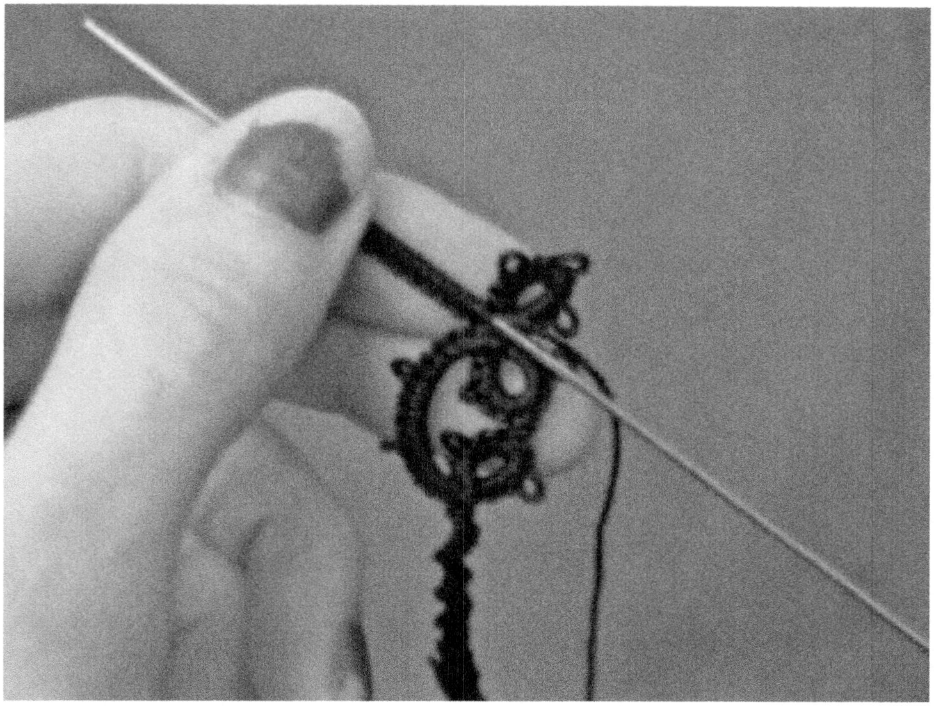

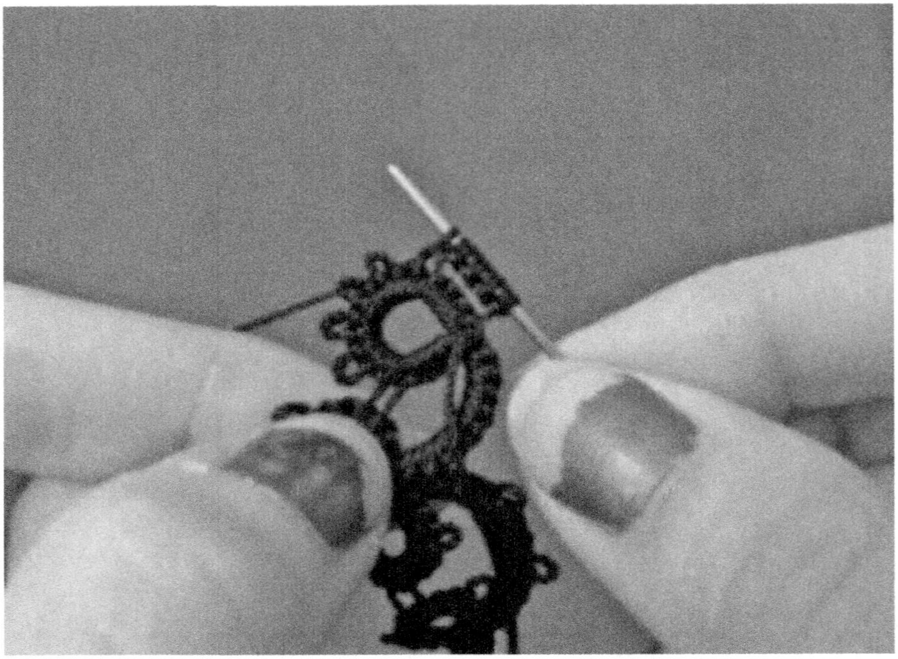

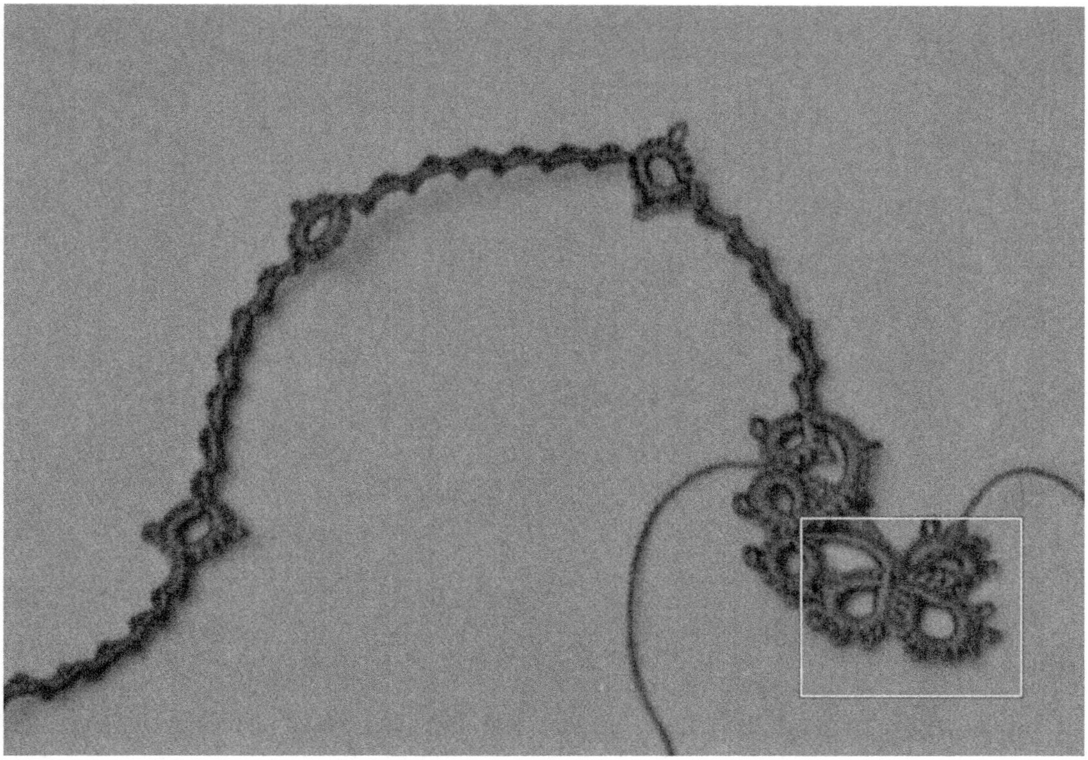

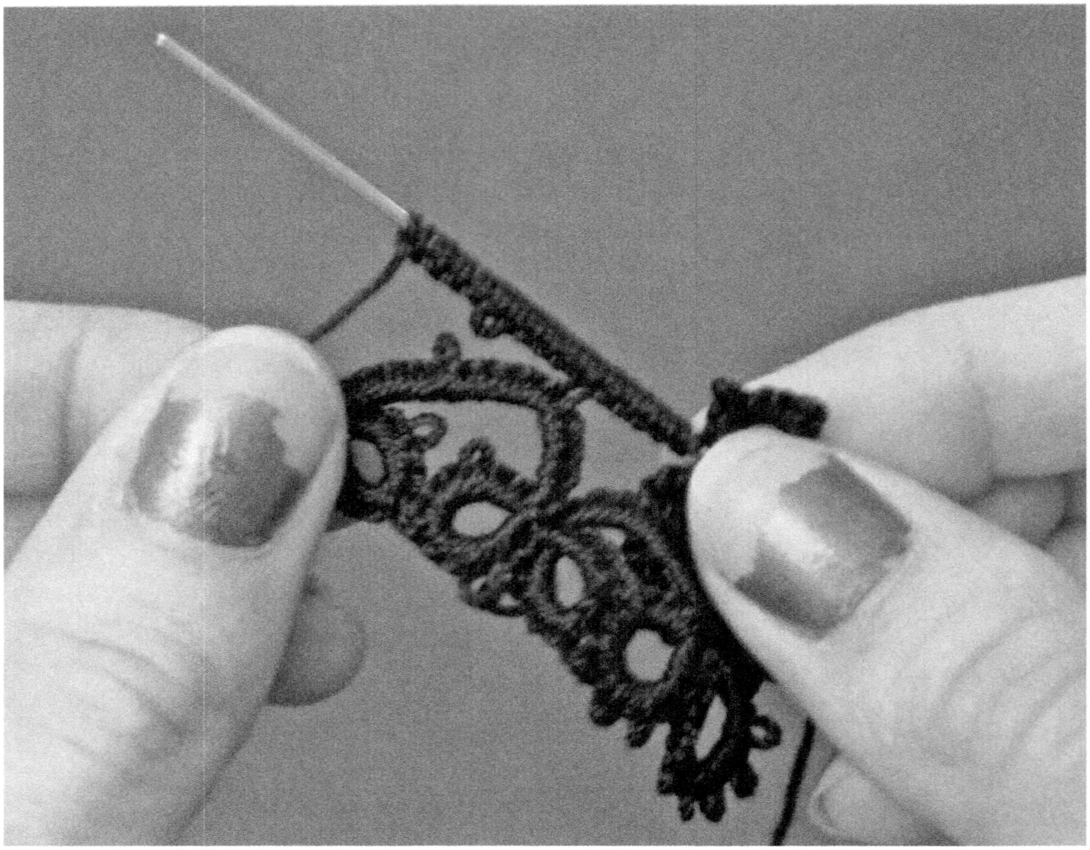

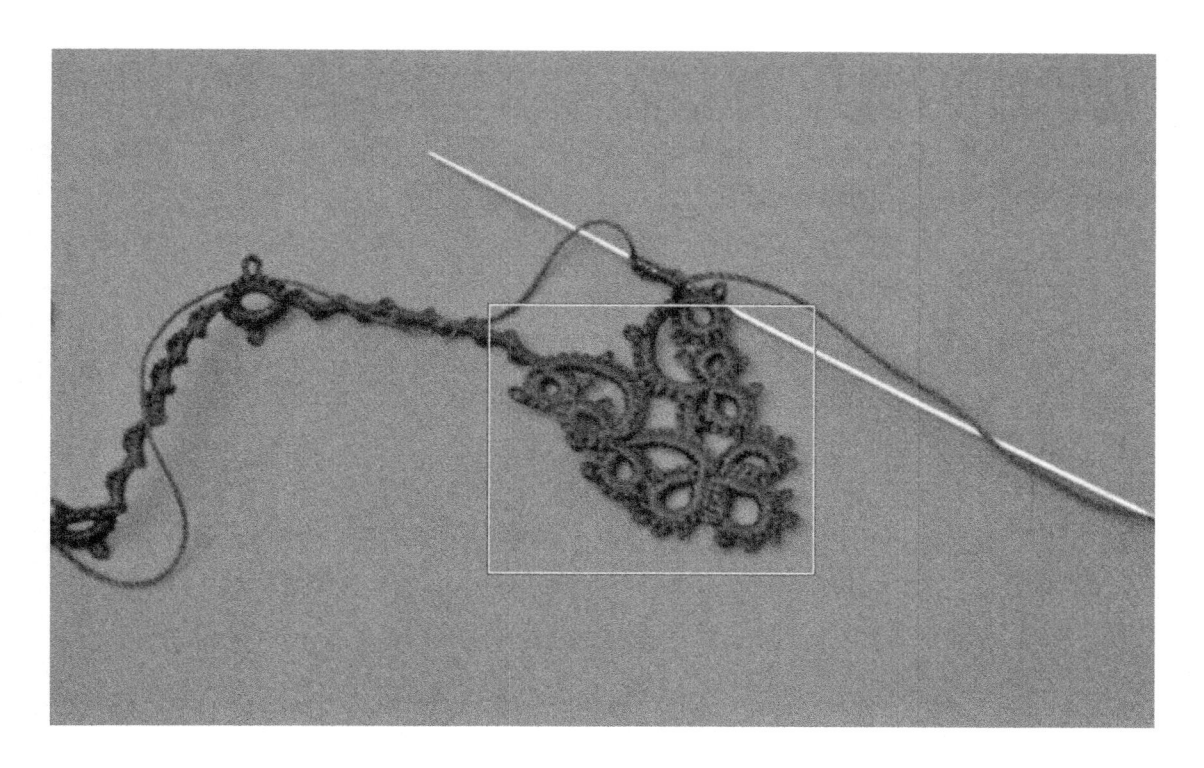

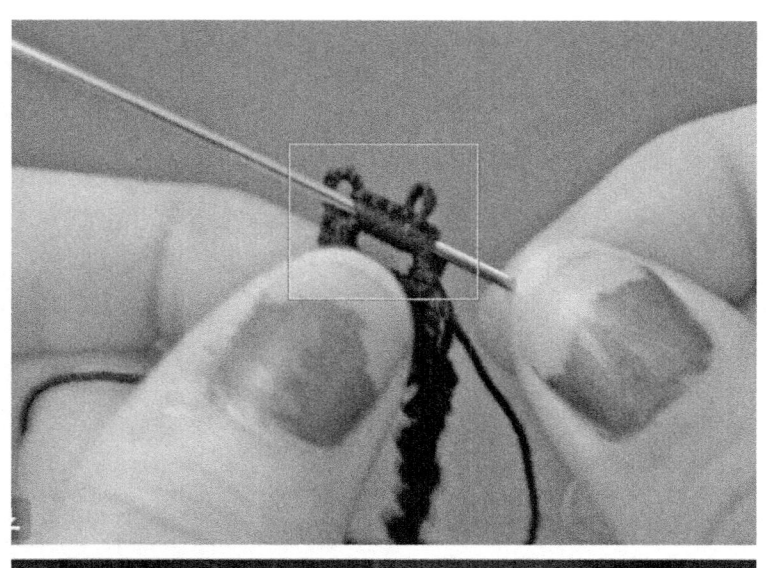

Introduction: Making a Necklace out of Needles

You are prepared to learn a few new methods if you have mastered the tatted flower tutorial. With the aid of this necklace, you may learn how to tat clovers, josephine knots, and split rings to make a wearable work of tatted art.

You will need to be familiar with the double stitch (ds), picots (p), rings (r), chains (ch), and joining, all of which can be learnt in my other instructional on needle tatting.

Size 10 crochet thread and a size 5 tatting needle were used for this pattern.

**Josephine Knot, first.**

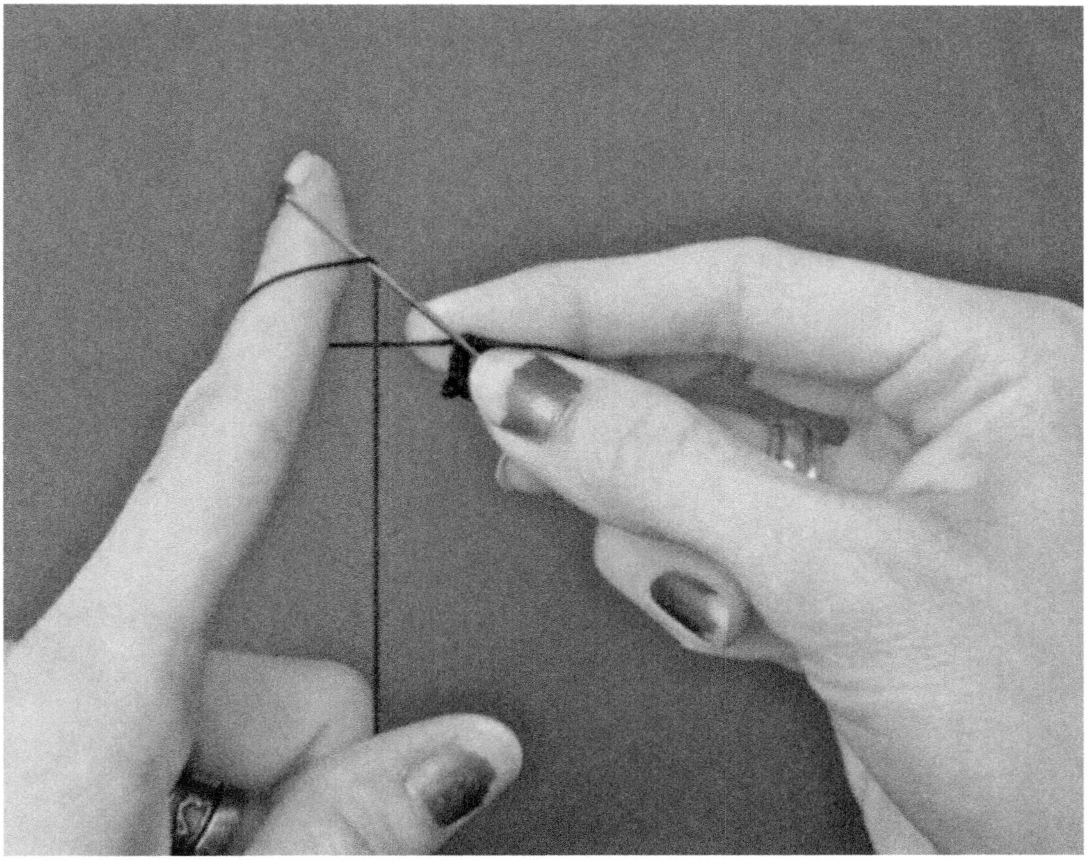

86

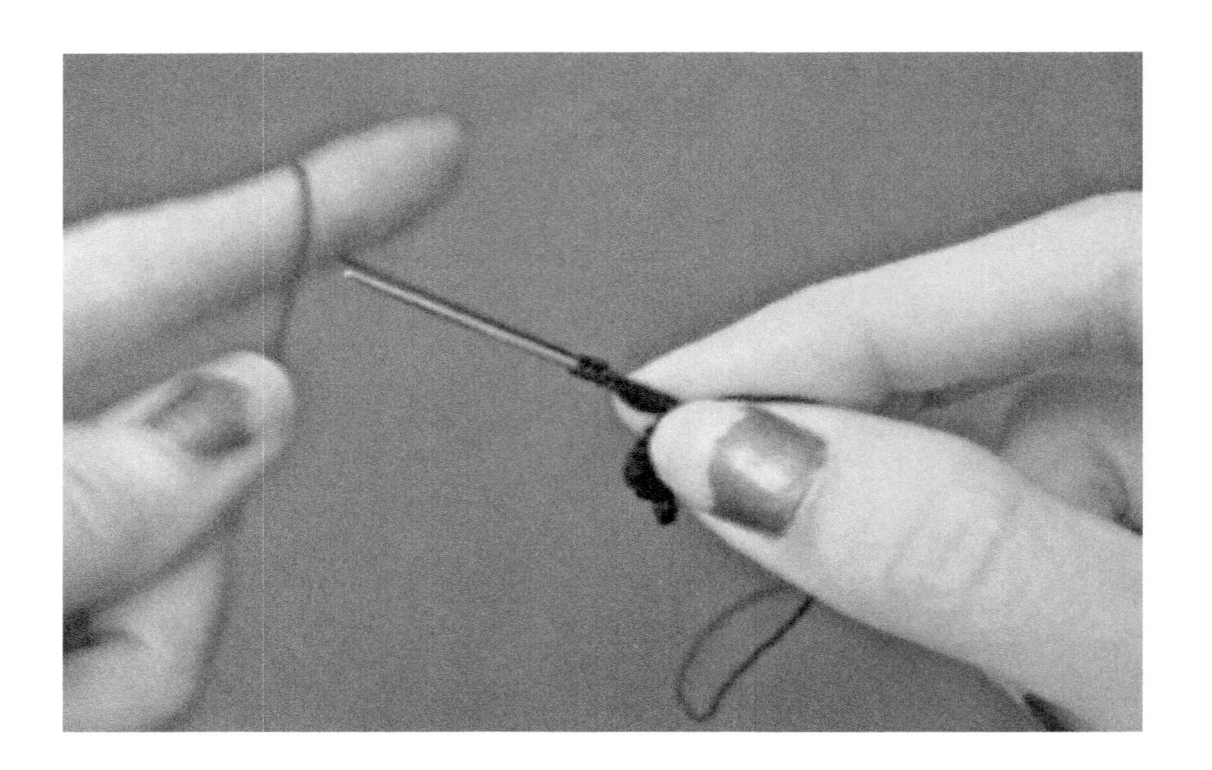

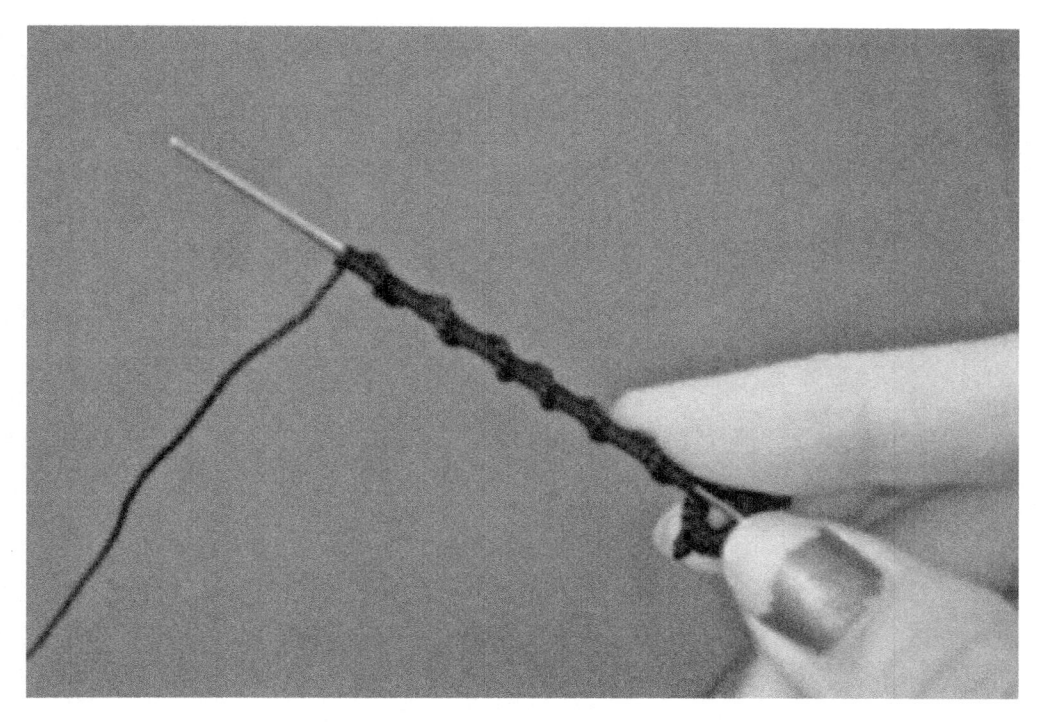

Start by threading your needle, leaving a tail of about six feet in the needle's eye.

1. Create a 3Ds ring. One point three times. Reverse and close work

The Josephine knot is made by repeatedly stitching the first half of a double stitch to form a spiral chain.

To keep an uniform spiral, you should take the thread up and around the needle every tenth stitch.

We'll create a chain of 60 Josephine knots for this pattern. As with a typical chain, pull the thread through the needle. Work in reverse and close.

**Next, split the ring.**

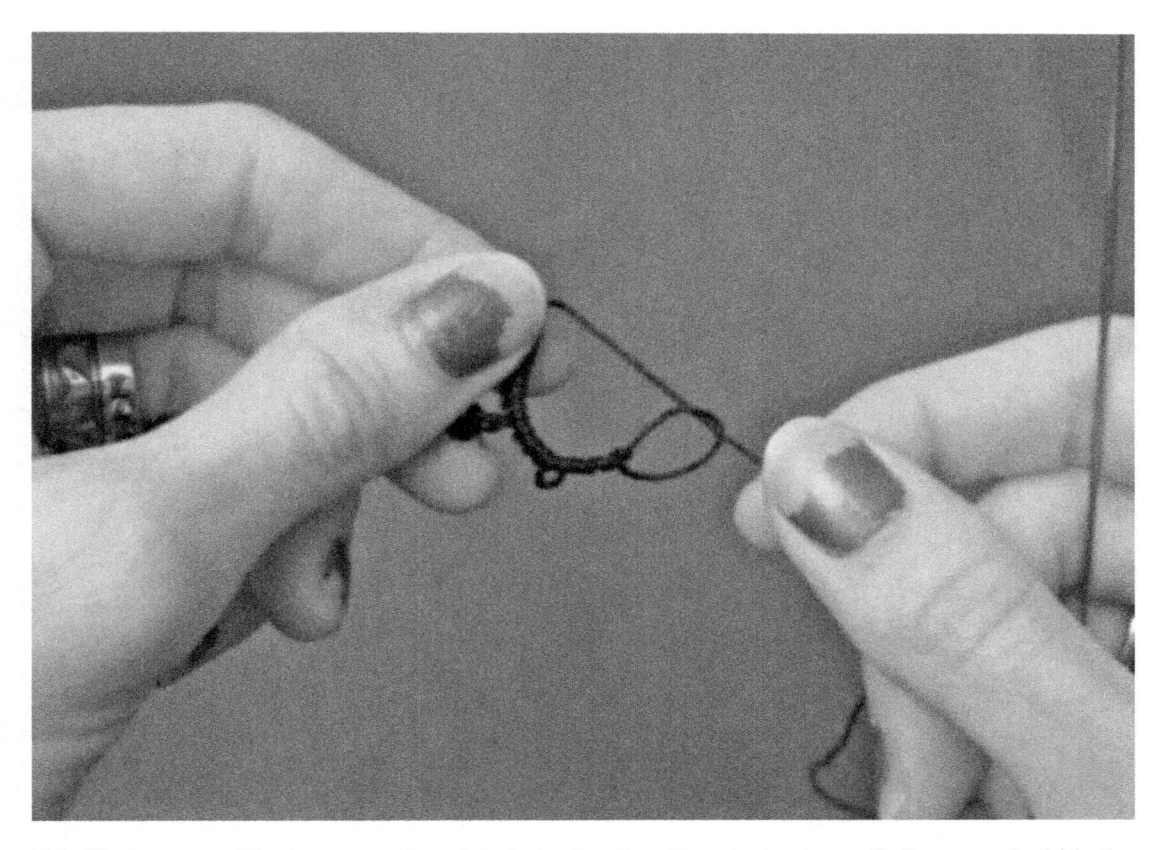

We'll do a split ring next, which is typically stated as follows: 4-4/4-4. the split-representing slash.

Tat 4ds 1p 4ds to begin the ring. The needle should then be unthreaded and turned around. With the tail thread, you will now tat. 1 p 4ds, then continue with 4ds.

Reverse the work, shut the ring like a regular ring, and rethread the needle.

**Third Step: The Chain**

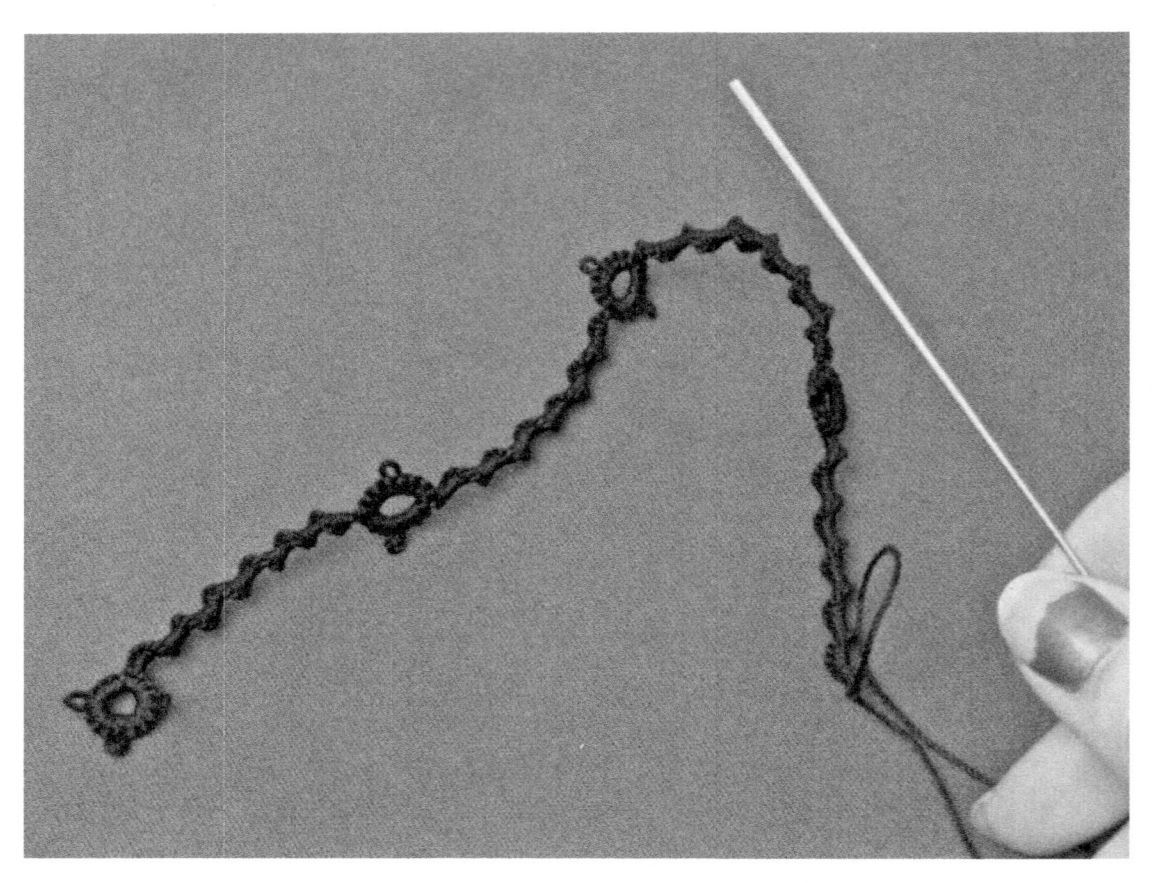

Work with split rings and Josephine Knot chains until you have four rings and four chains altogether, including the first one you produced.

**Fourth Step: The Pendant**

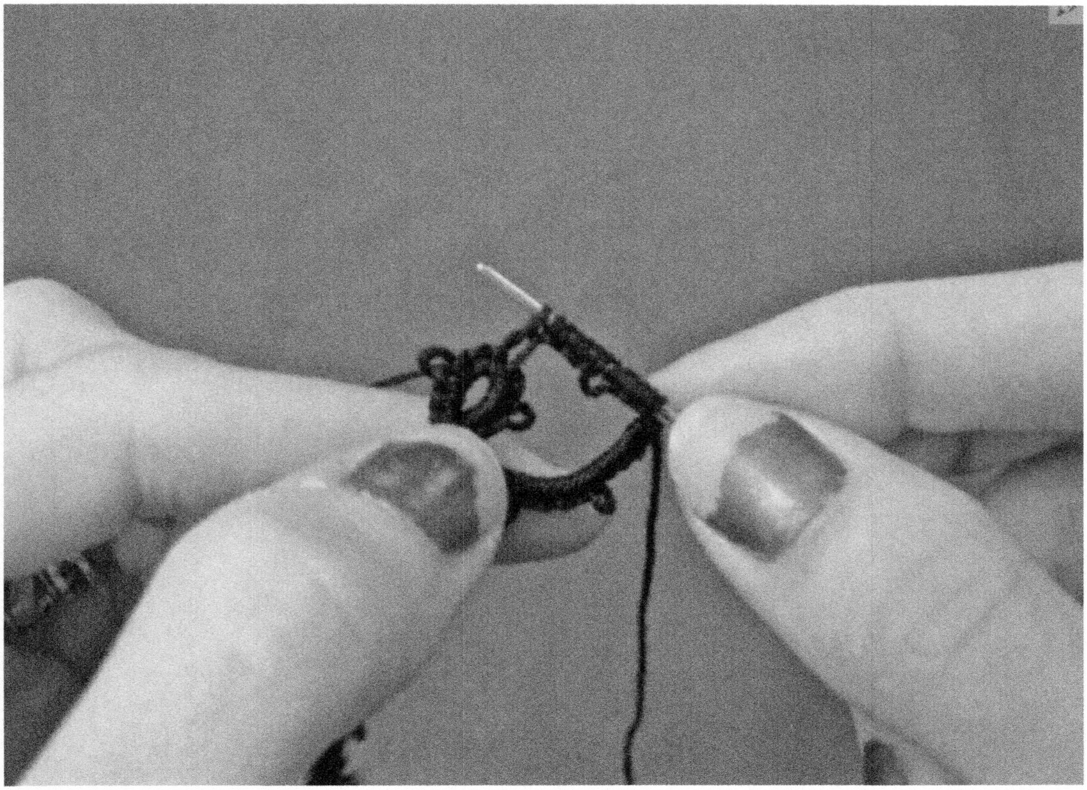

The necklace's primary pendant section is now being constructed.

1. Close rw R 3ds 1p 3ds 1p 3ds 1p 3ds
2. Ch 1p 1p 5ds near rw
3. R 3ds 1p 3ds join to last ring's center picot. R 3ds 1p 3ds close.
4. R3ds1p3ds1p3ds1p3ds cl rw
5. Ch 10 cl rw

**Fifth step: Clover motif**

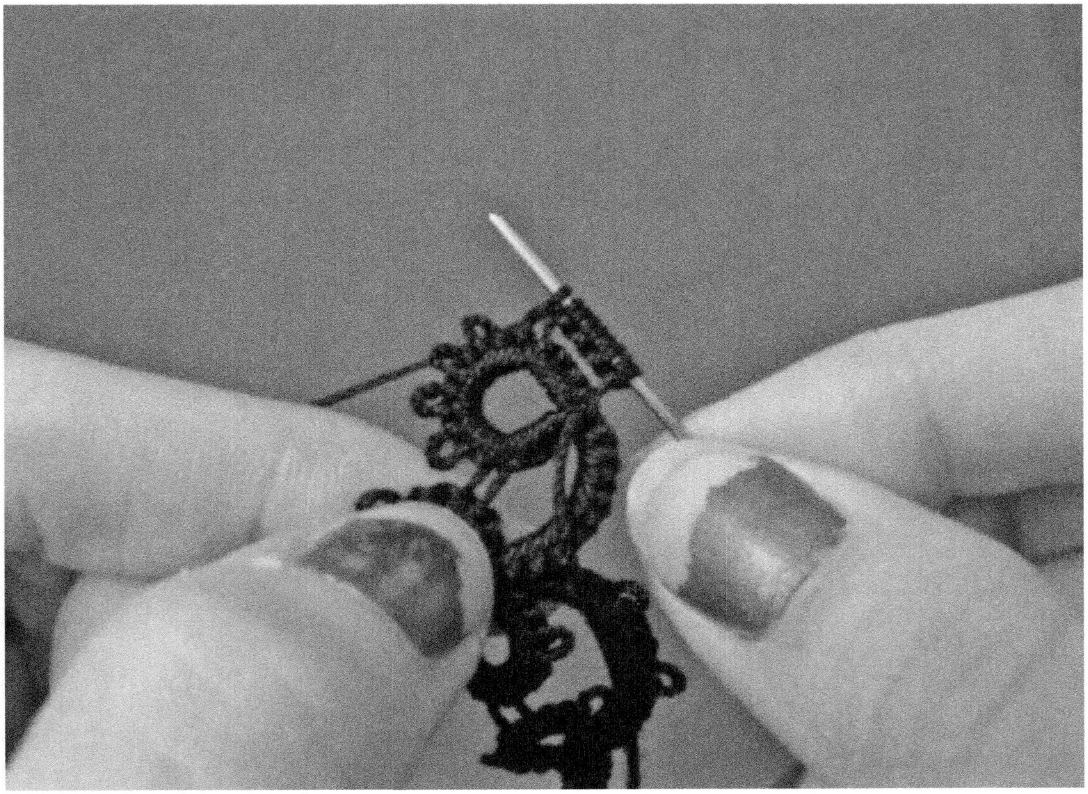

The clover is one of the most often used tatting patterns; although having a wide range of stitch counts, they are all built in the same way.


1.R 4ds attach to preceding ring 2ds center picot, 1p 2ds, 1p 2ds, 1p 4ds, close REMOVE WORK REVERSING

2. R 4ds attach to previous ring's last picot with ring 2ds, 1p 2ds, 1p 2ds, 1p 2ds, and 1p 4ds. REMOVE WORK REVERSING

3. R 4ds link to previous ring's last picot. R 2ds, 1p 2ds, 1p 2ds, 1p 4ds close. rw

**Clover completed, step 6: complete pendant**

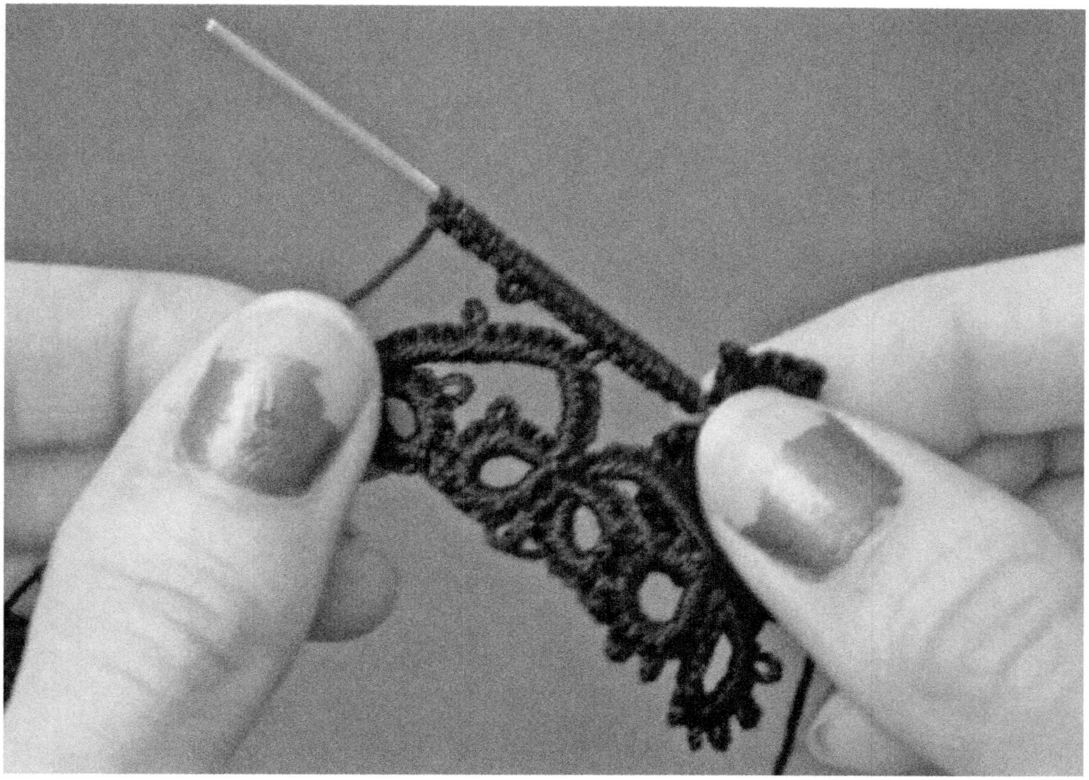

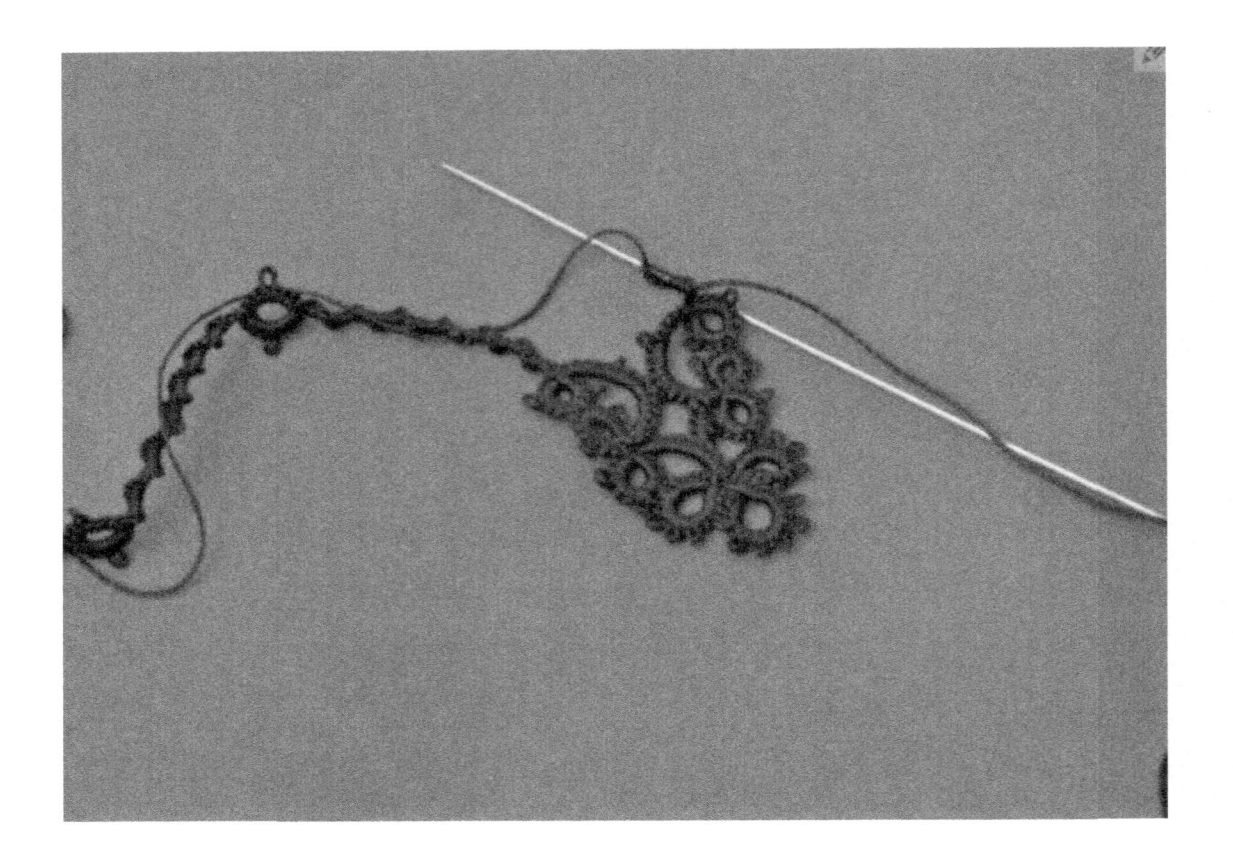

Work on the second side in the same manner as the first.

Ch. 10 cl. rw

2. Do not reverse work; R 3ds 1p 3ds join to final picot of the previous ring.

3. R 3ds 1p 1p 1p 1p 3ds cl rw

4. Ch 5 join to opposite chain's picot with 5ds 1p 5ds cl rw.

5. R 3ds 1p 3ds attach to the previous ring's middle ring.

**Step 7: Finish the second chain.**

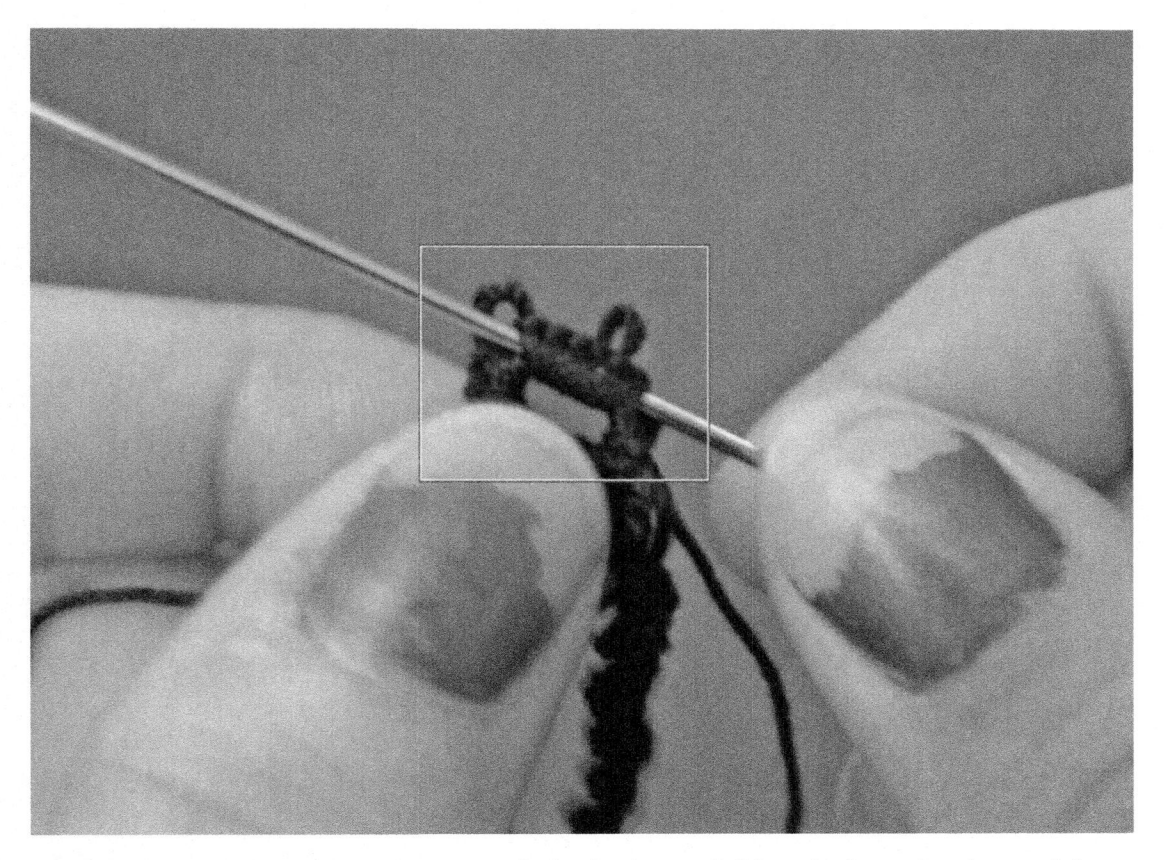

With a total of 3 split rings and 4 chains of 60 stitches in Josephine knots, work the second chain in the same manner as the first.

Finish with a ring made of 4ds 1p 4ds 1p 4ds 1p 4ds, tightly knot the ends in a double knot, and then tuck them inside the last ring.

After applying steam to the completed item, add the desired clasp to the ends by using the picots to secure them.

Now that you know how to do it, you may change the pendant or central motif, as well as the chains and split rings, to make any type of necklace you choose.

**CHAPER SEVEN**

# HOW TO USE A NEEDLE FOR TATTING

What You Will Need

• Thread \s• Needle

For the greatest tatting results, the sizes of the needle and thread should be comparable.

Tatting is a method for making ornamental doilies and lace edging by tying loops and knots. Tatting can be identified by the little rings or arched chains woven into the lace. The technique uses typically white or off-white colors, and it was a popular pastime in the middle of the 19th century. A very tiny thread to one that is a little heavier can be used, depending on the application. A shuttle, a tool with an integrated hook, can also be used for tatting.

Because of a problem with your internet connection, this video cannot be played.

First, make a thread piece that is at least 40 inches long. Through the needle's eye, thread the material. The length of one end should be approximately four inches, while the length of the other side should be at least 36 inches.

**Step 2:** Take the needle and hold it in your right hand. Utilizing the left hand, move the longer piece of thread under the needle. Keep the thread close to the needle. The longer strand of thread should be wrapped around the left hand's bottom three fingers.

**Step 3:** Circumferentially wrap the thread around the finger. Move the needle up until the tip of the index finger is where it should be. Thread should be wound around the needle. Once finished, take off the finger.

**Step 4:** Holding the thread with your index finger, secure the stitch on the needle. Around the index finger, wrap the piece of thread anticlockwise. As you bend the finger, the needle will move up to the fingertip.

**Step 5:** Slide the second stitch to fit against the first stitch by moving the thread down the needle one more. Repeat the procedure, transferring each finished stitch to the needle's tip.

**Tip**

Reverse the instructions to use your left hand instead of your right if you are a left-handed person.

### How to Tie a Knot and Thread a Needle

What You Will Need

Sharp scissors, sewing needles, and thread

### How to Tie a Knot and Thread a Needle

Threading the needle is one of the initial processes in hand sewing. It will only take a little time and practice to master this technique, which has been passed down through the years, before you can tie a knot while closing your eyes. You can require a single strand of thread or two, depending on your job. Just one end of the thread should be knotted when stitching with a single strand. Put a knot in both ends to create a double strand. For quilting, embroidery, and sewing hems, use a single strand. For stitching seams, snaps, or buttons, use a double strand.

**Resources Step 1**

**What You Will Need**

Choose the right sewing supplies for your project, such as a large-eye needle and a "between" needle for hand quilting or six-strand floss and a "between" needle for embroidery. An itemized list of tools and materials can be seen on the last slide.

**Step 2**

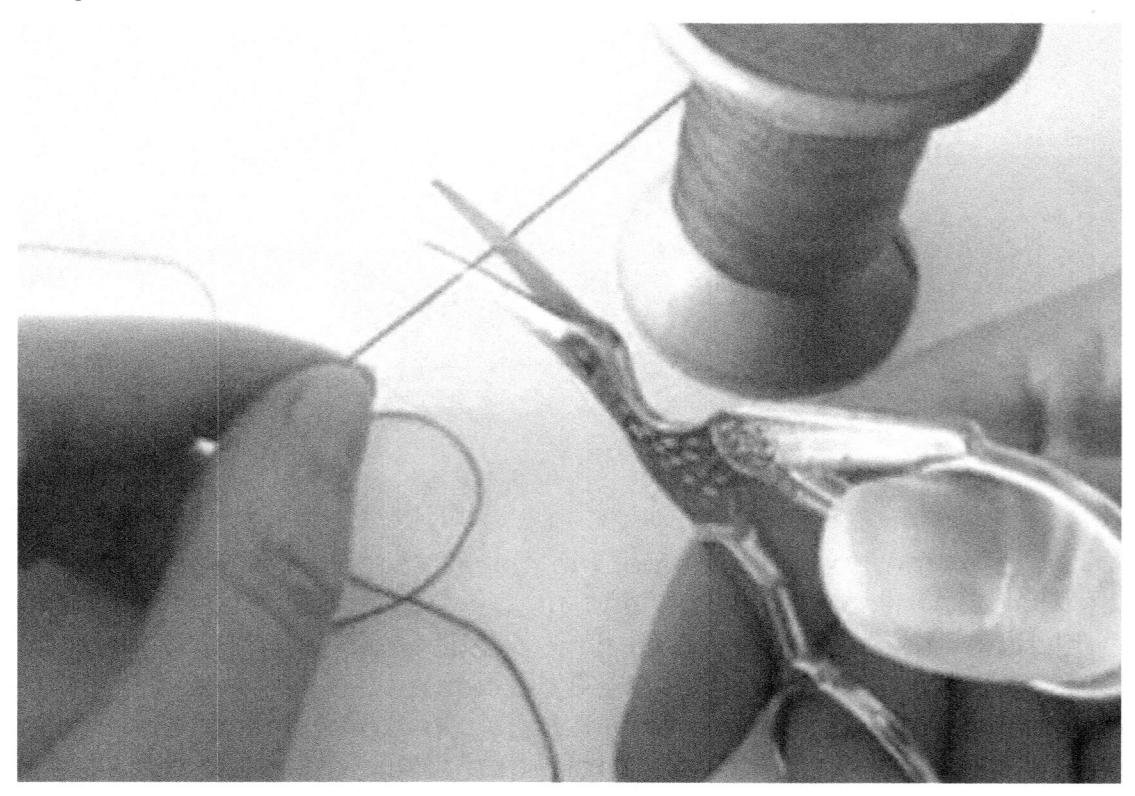

Trim a piece of thread.

For a single strand, cut a length of thread approximately 18 inches, and for a double strand, about 36 inches. Although longer pieces can appear more practical, they often tangle as you sew.

**Step 3**

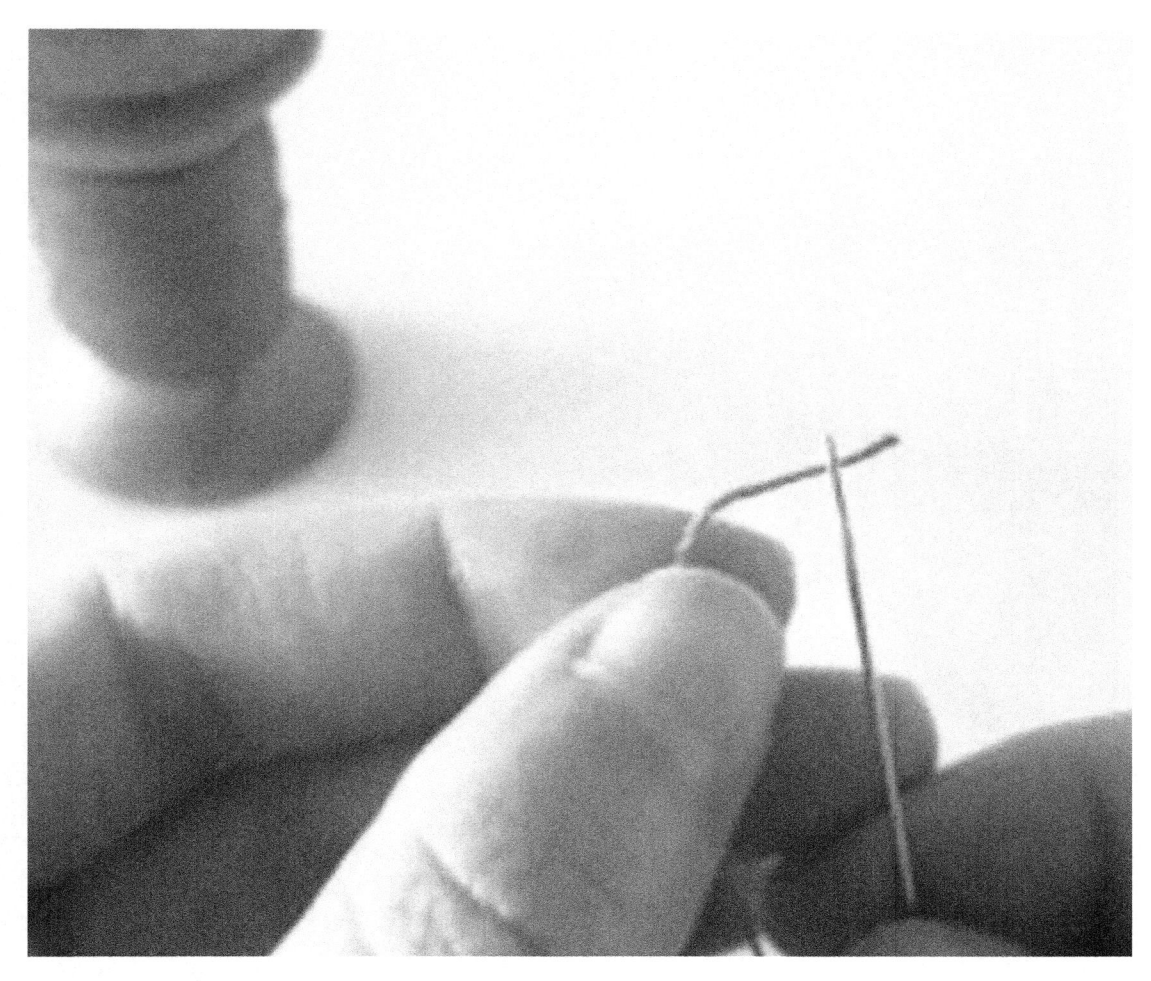

needle threading

To make a sharp tip, wet one end of the thread with your lips. Slowly pass the thread through the needle's eye while holding the needle in one hand and the thread in the other.

**Step 4**

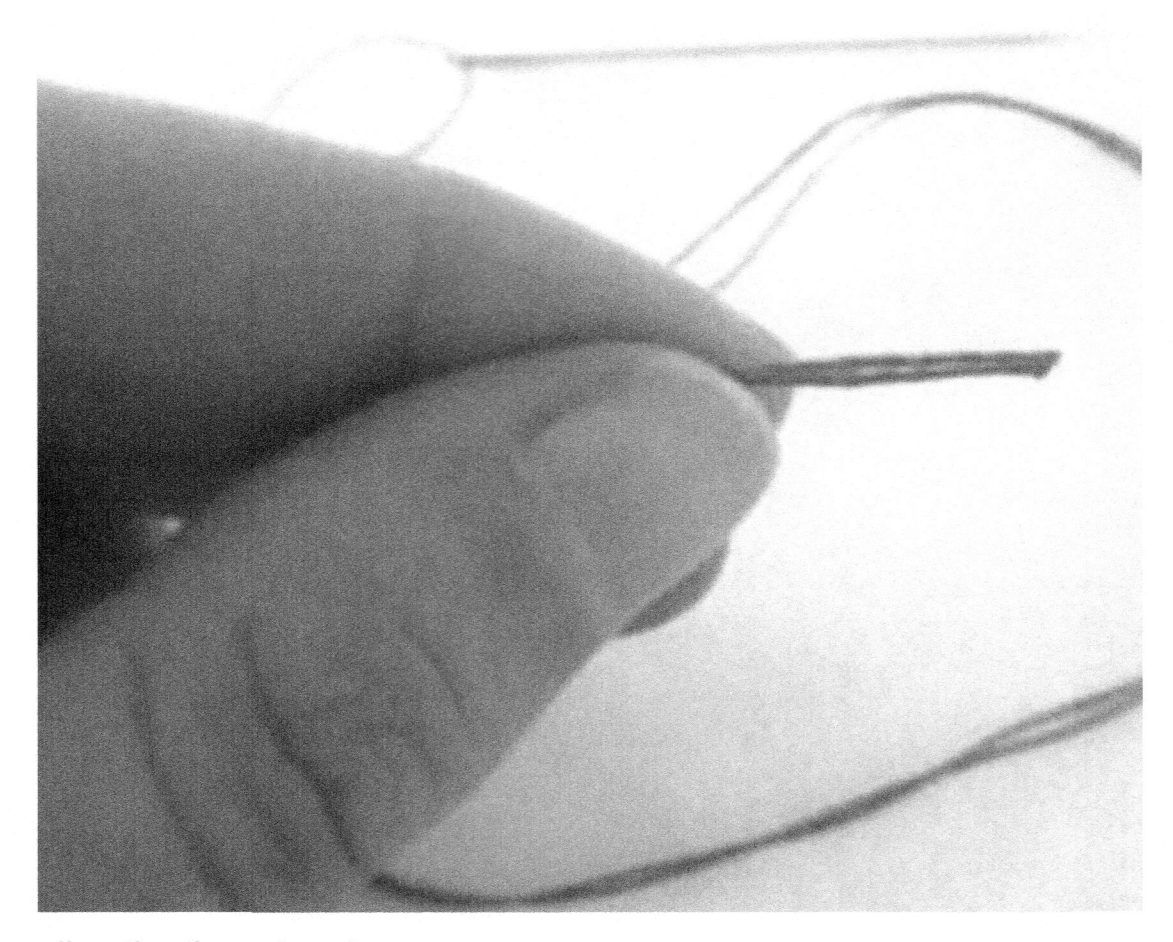

align the thread ends.

Picture Source: Amelia Strader

Pull around 6 inches of thread through the eye to create a single strand. Arrange the ends in a double strand.

**Step 5**

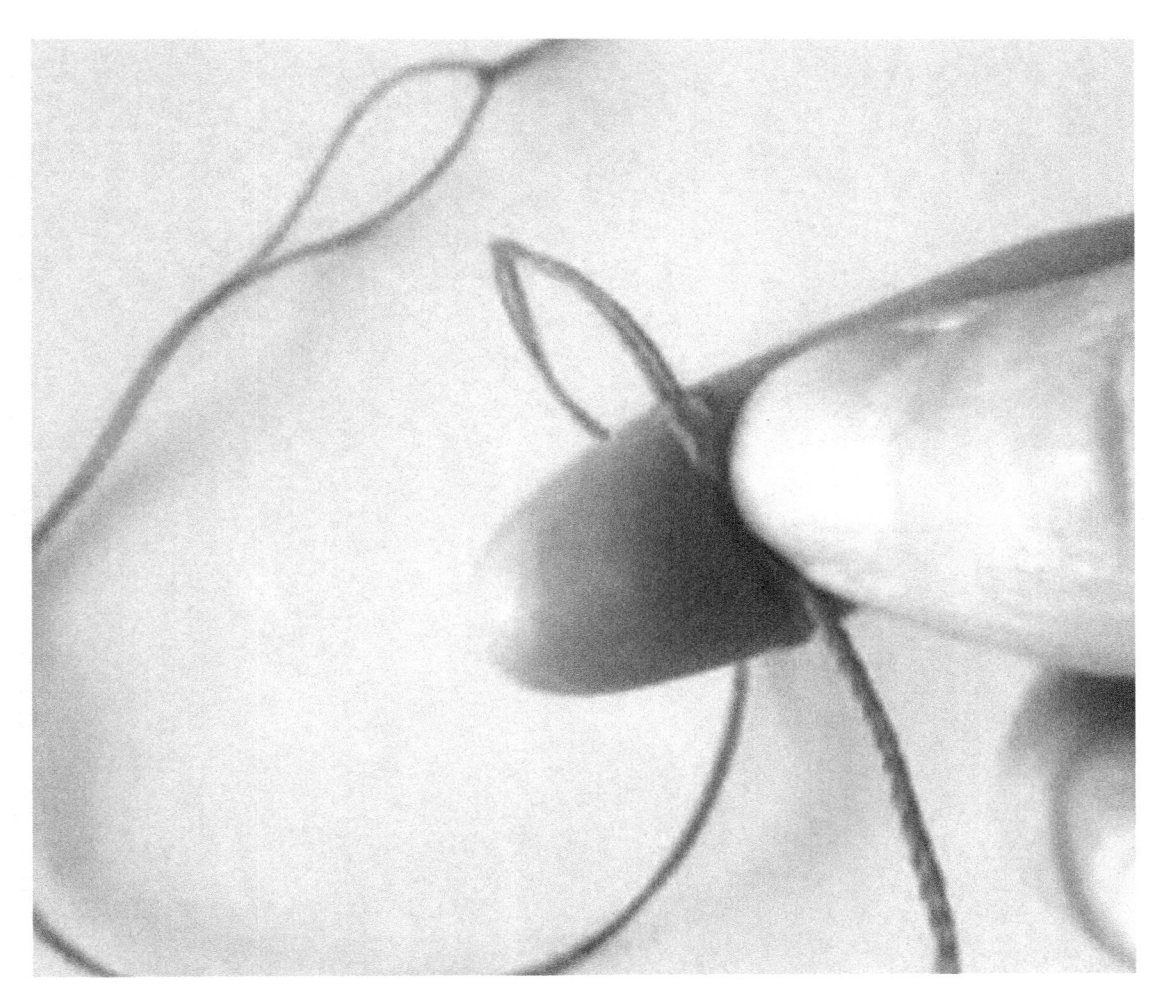

Set up a loop.

One time around the tip of your index finger, wrap the thread, and secure with your thumb.

**Step 6**

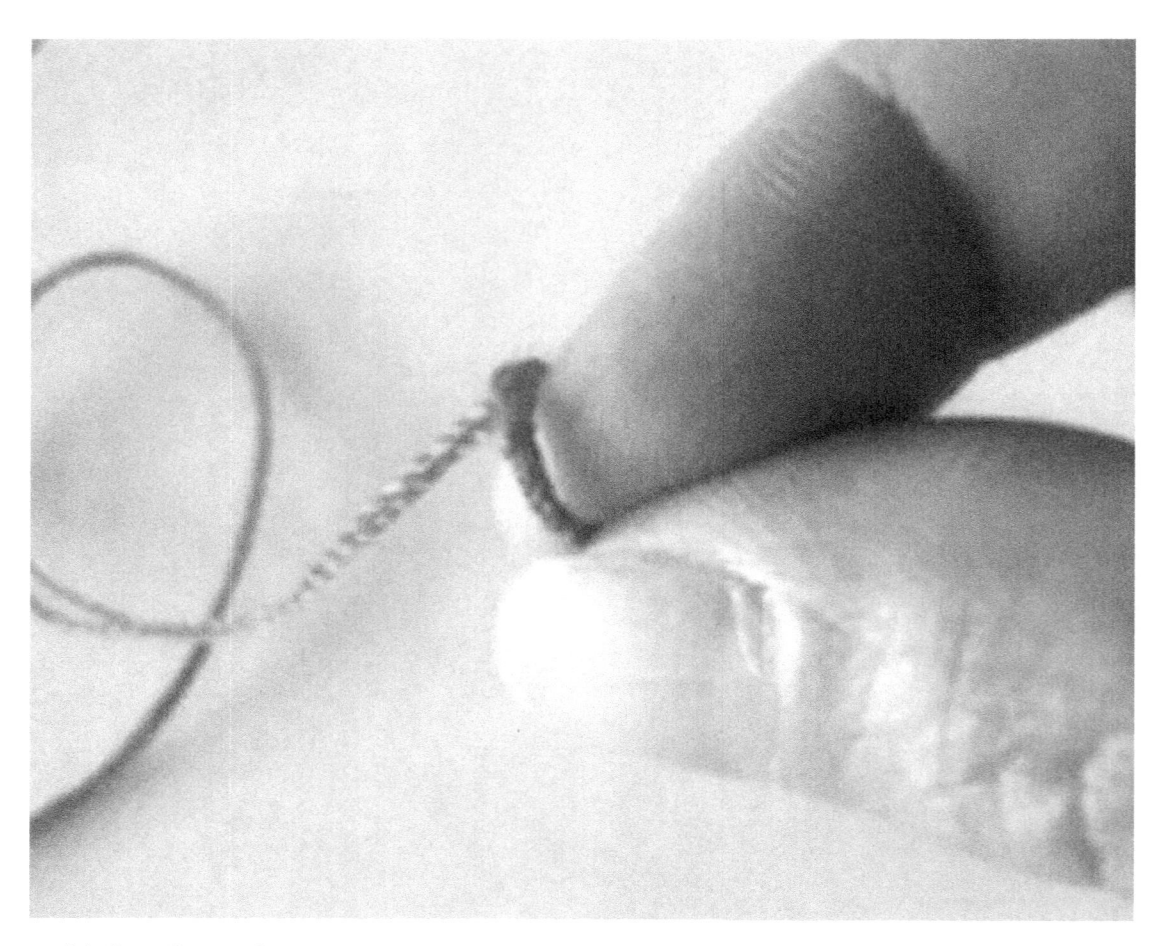

twirl the thread.

Picture Source: Amelia Strader

Between your index finger and thumb, turn the thread forward.

**Step 7**

Enlarge the loop.

Making a loop, slide the thread off your index finger.

**Step 8**

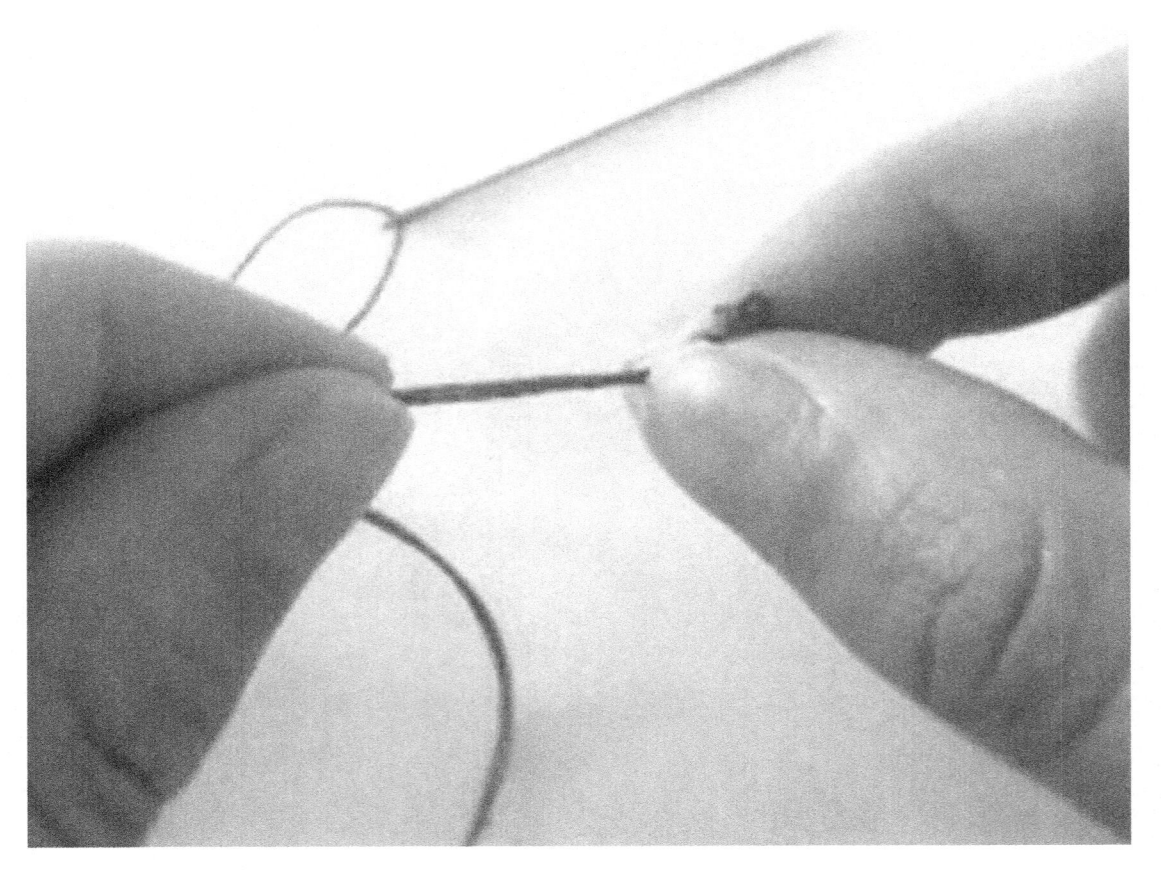

tuck the thread loop away.

Picture Source: Amelia Strader

While maintaining a firm grip on the thread with your other hand, hold the loop loosely between your index finger and thumb. To tighten the loop and create a knot, pull downward with your thumb and index finger.

**Step 9**

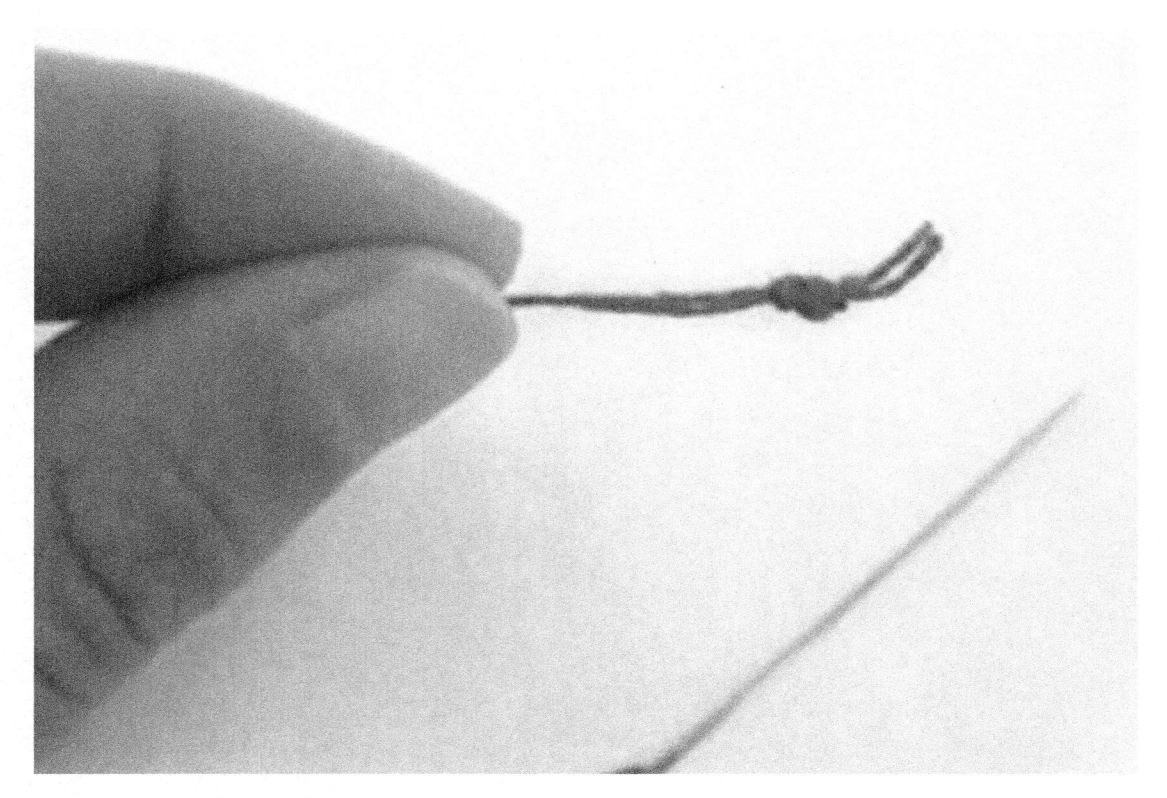

If needed, cut the ends.

## CHAPTER EIGHT LEARN NEEDLEWORK USING MY FLOWER PENDANT

My mask is certainly cool, but it is not for beginners. This is an introductory needle tatting project. This simple floral pendant will teach you some needle tatting fundamentals. No prior knowledge of tatting is required, however familiarity with other fiber arts, such as knitting and crochet, may aid comprehension of pattern development.

You will need a tatting needle of size 5 and crochet cotton thread of size 10. Though using any thread and needle will result in blooms of varying sizes.

This is not an exhaustive manual for needle tatting. This craft will show you how to work with thread on a ball, which resembles tatting with two shuttles. In addition to working with cut thread to imitate one shuttle tatting, you can also master numerous more sophisticated techniques.

**First Step: Part 1 of the Double Stitch**

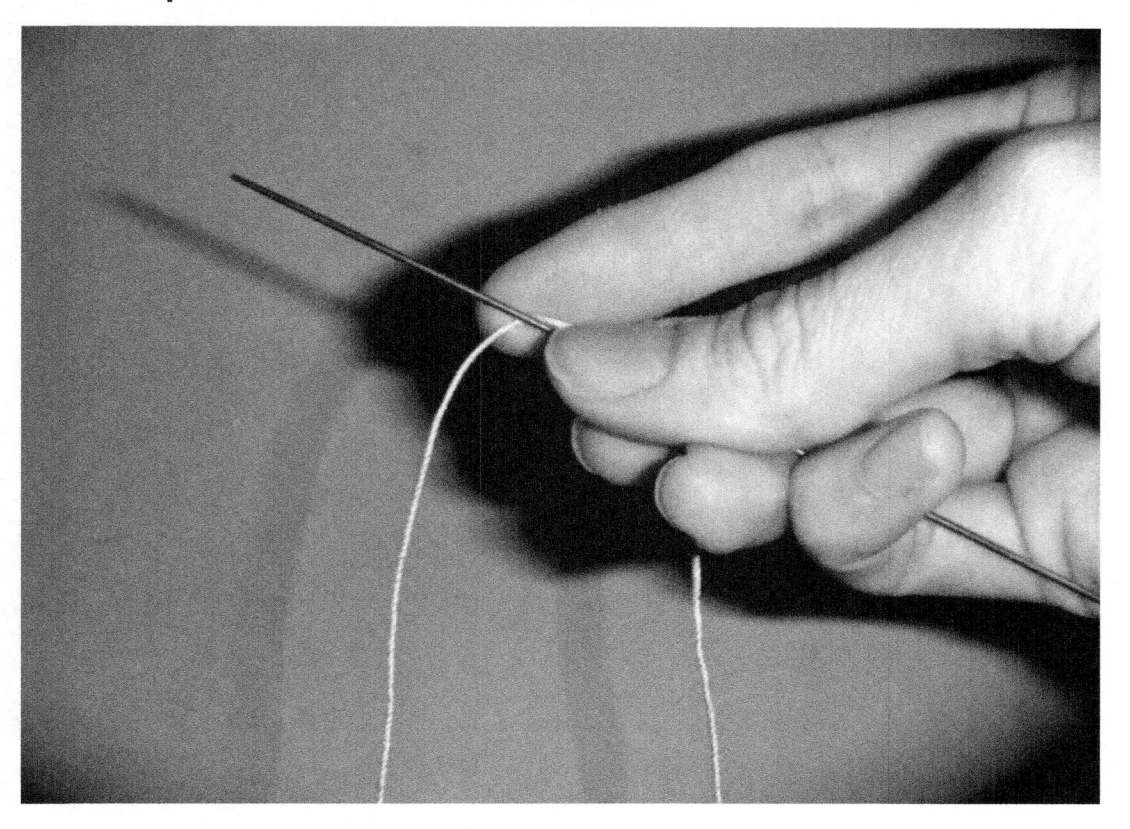

Tatting typically consists of a single stitch, with double stitches divided by picots. This stitch is used to create the rings and chains that comprise tatting's primary structure.

1. Thread yarn from the ball onto the needle, leaving a 16-inch tail.

2. Hold the working thread (thread from the ball, not the tail) close to the end of the needle with the index finger on your right hand. When the initial ds has been formed, you may release the thread.

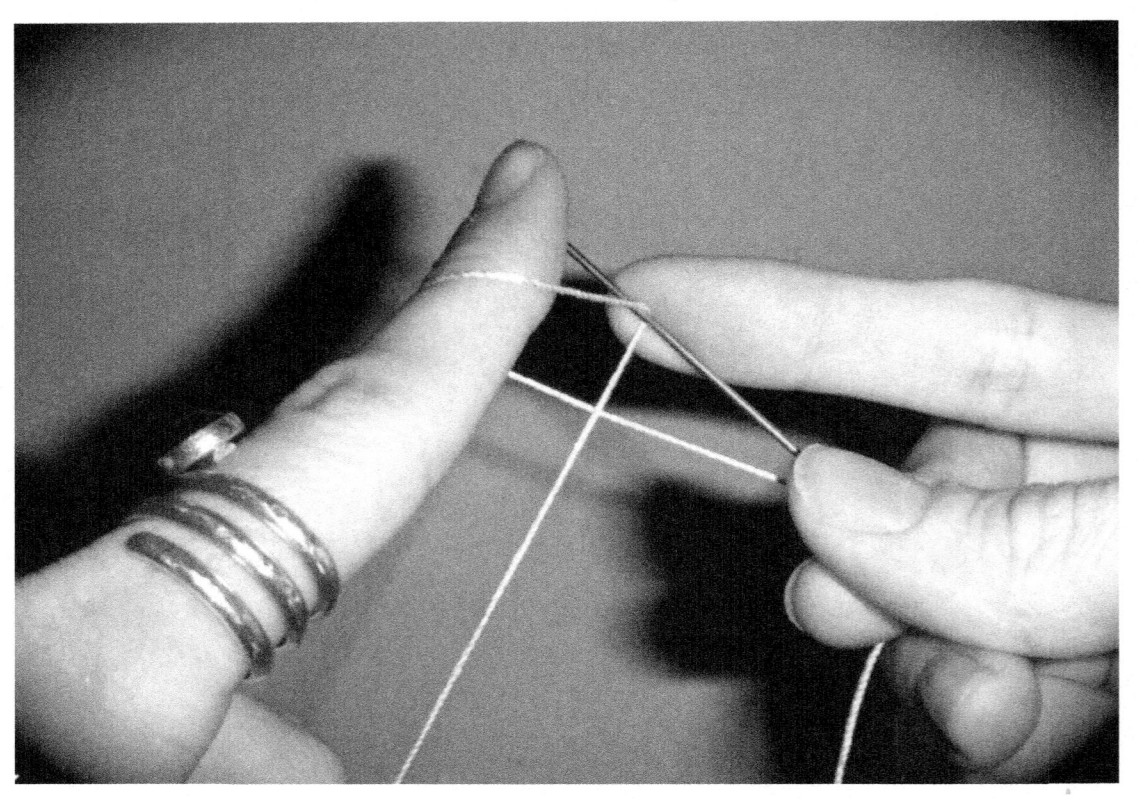

**The First Half of the Double Stitch, Step 2**

1. While holding the thread with your other three fingers, wrap the thread around the back of your index finger in a clockwise direction.

Slide the needle under the thread and up toward the fingertip. Remove finger and pull the loop onto the needle until it is snug. This is the beginning of the ds

**Step 3: The remainder of the Double Stitch**

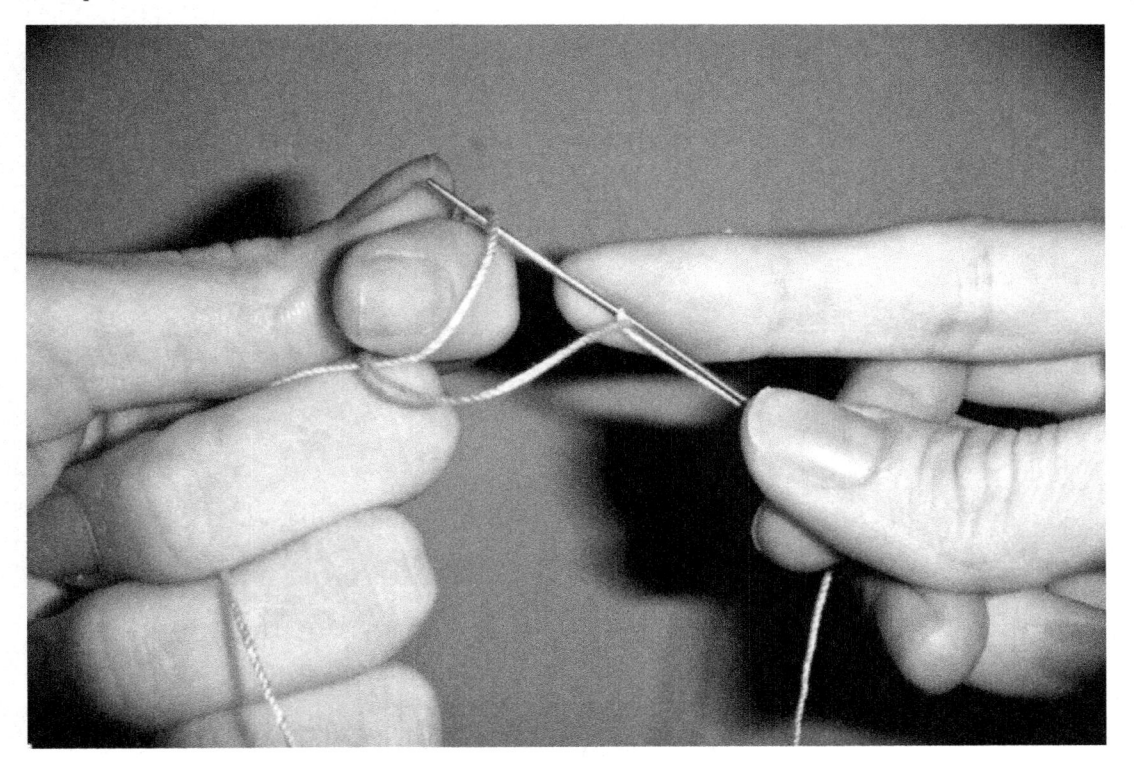

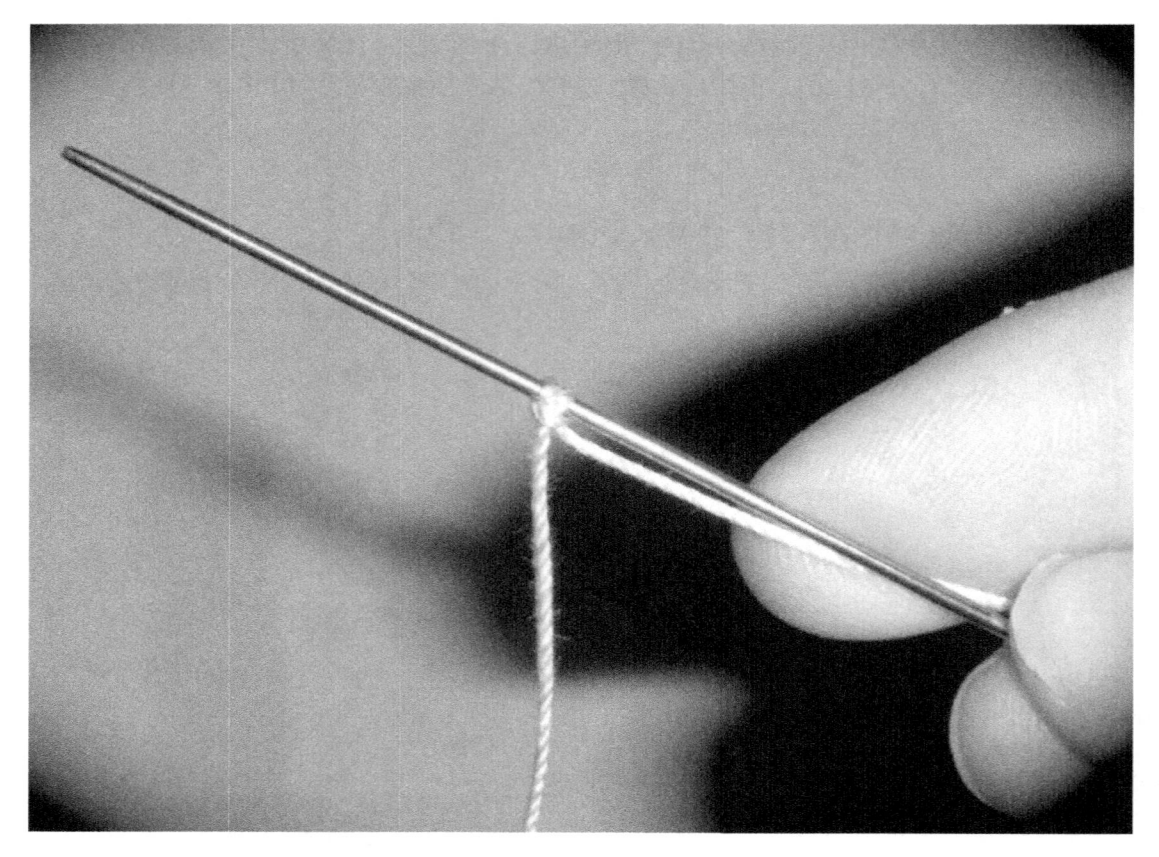

For the remainder of the ds, we take the opposite approach. Wind the thread counter-clockwise around your index finger, then move the needle under the thread toward the tip of your finger. Place the second loop adjacent to the first and tighten.

You may observe that this is merely a half hitch knot.

**Fourth Step: Creating a Picot**

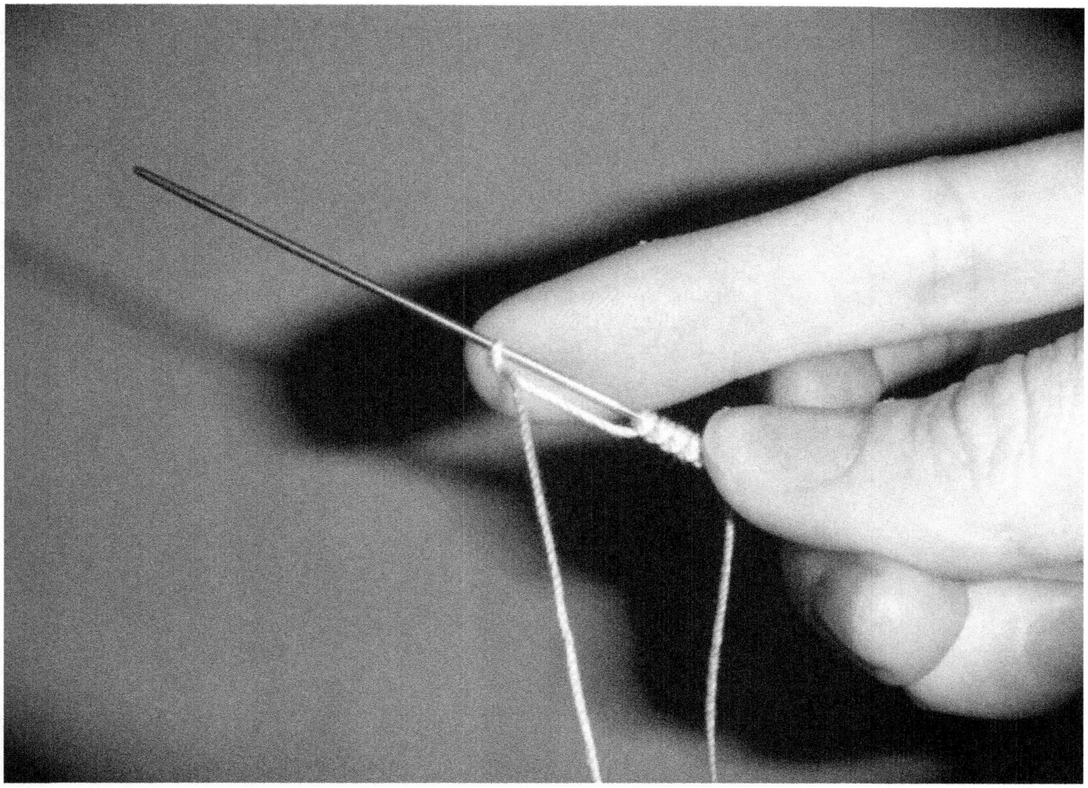

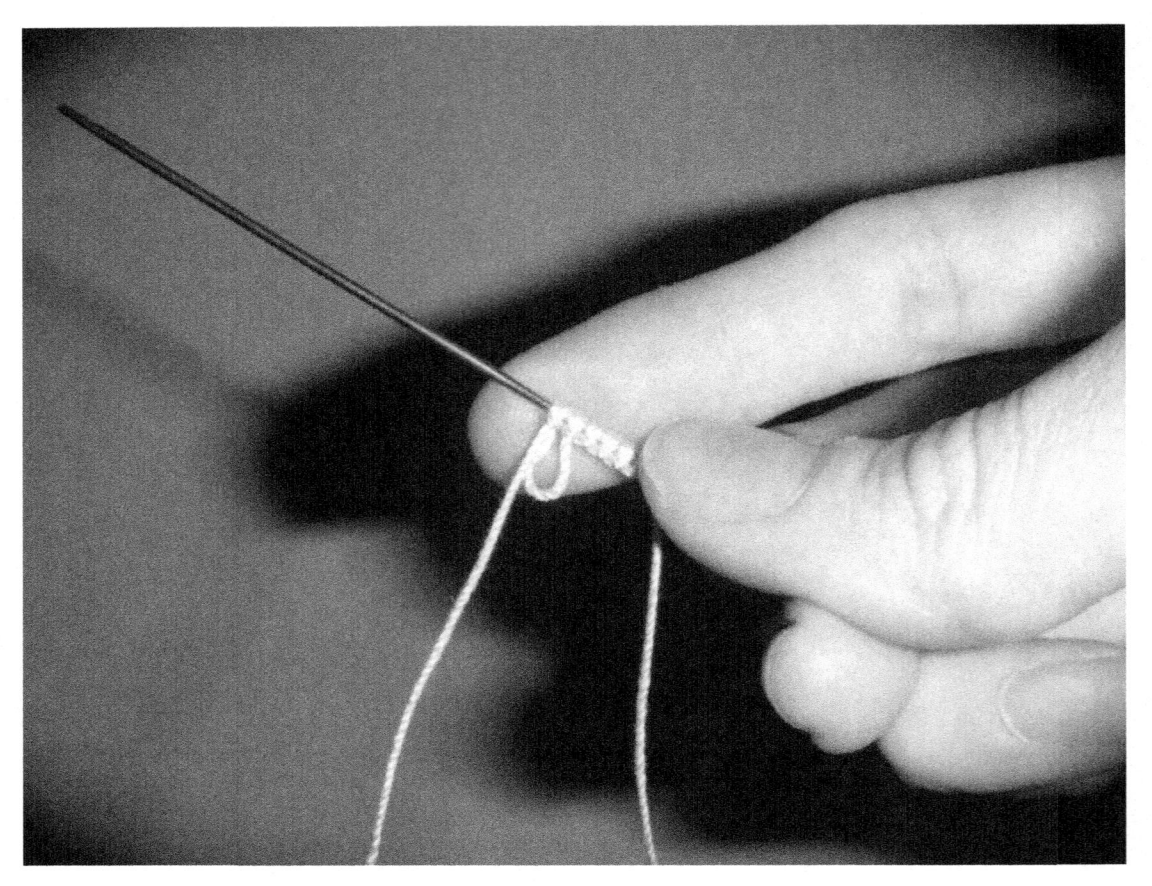

1. After finishing a ds, build the first half of the next ds, but instead of sliding the loop next to the first ds, hold it approximately 1/2 inch apart while completing the second half of the ds.

Slide the completed ds alongside the initial ds. The tiny loop formed between them is known as a Picot.

**The fifth step is to create a ring.**

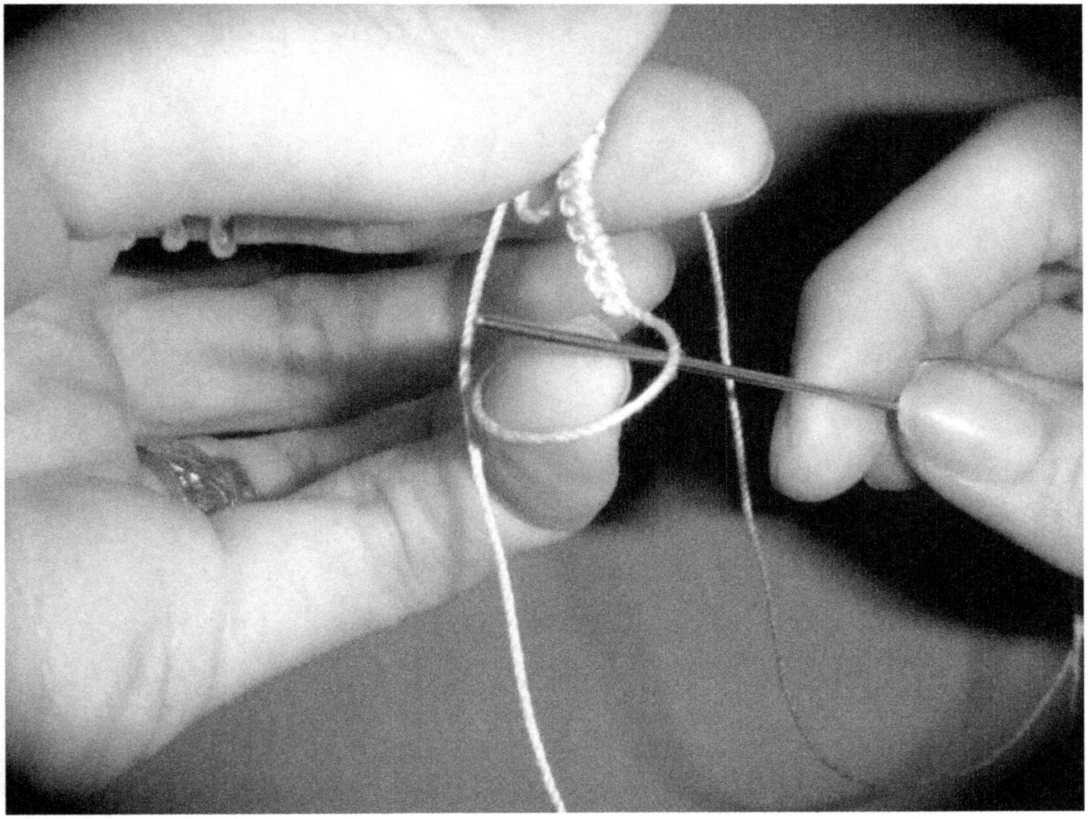

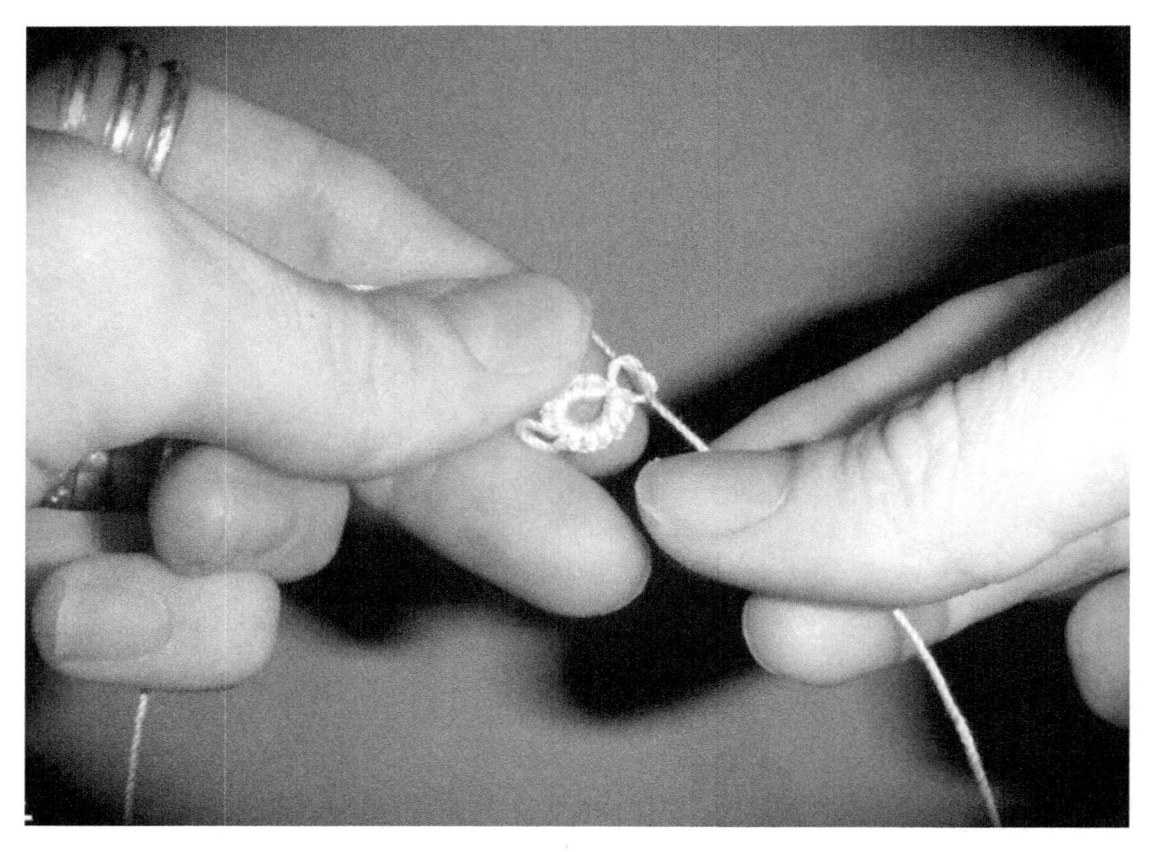

Create any number of double crochets with any number of picots. For our floral pendant, construct a ring of six double crochets followed by a long picot (1 inch) and six more double crochets.

2. Slide the ds off the needle and onto the thread in the eye of the needle, preventing the loop from closing by inserting your pinky inside the loop.

Bring the needle's point through the loop and pull it closed. In written patterns, this is termed "closing the ring."

The final step involves flipping the ring over and tying a knot at the top. This is known as rw or reverse work.

## Sixth Action: Creating a Chain

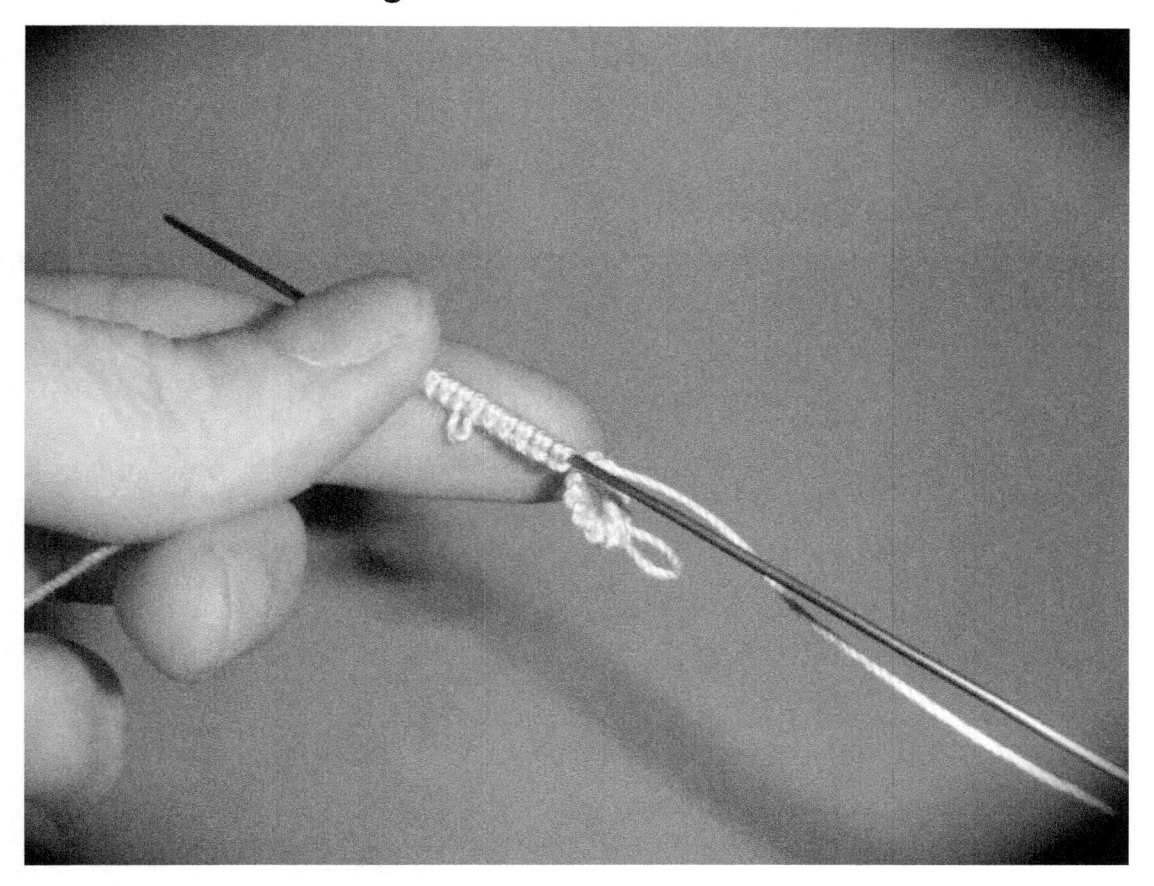

Place the needle at the final knot on the ring. Typically, a chain is formed only after a ring.

Create as many ds and picots as desired. For our floral pendant, you will need chain 6ds, 1 picot(p), and 6 ds.

Slide the ds from the eye of the needle onto the thread in the eye. Pull the thread completely through so that the chain is immediately adjacent to the ring.

As with the ring, flip the chain over and secure it with a knot (rw). Occasionally, after closing, a ring or chain is not reversed, but a knot is still made. The right and left threads do not switch positions when this knot is tied.

**Step 7: Flower Creation**

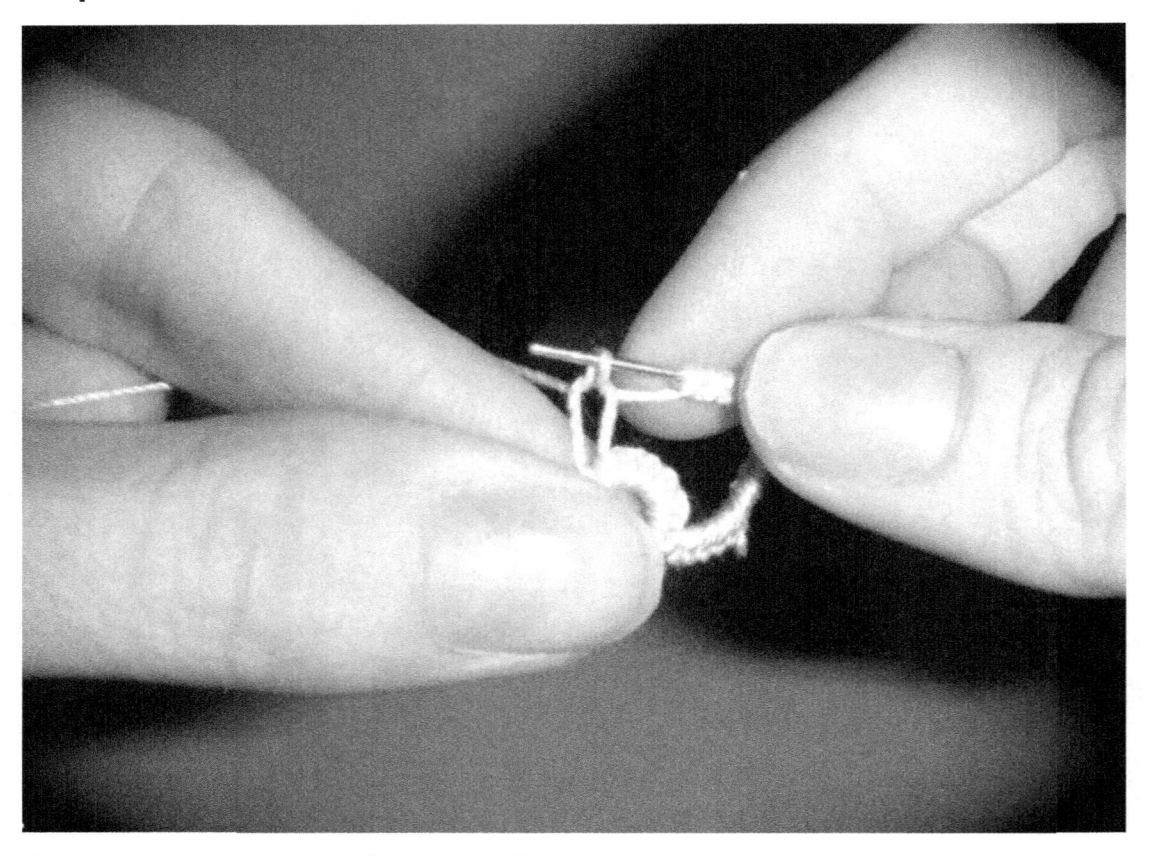

Continue making the flower until you have one ring and one chain.

1. Make a 6-ds ring and attach it to the long picot of the first ring by pulling the working thread through the picot with the tip of the needle. Complete the ring using 6ds, close, and rw.

Next, build another chain consisting of 6ds, 1p, 6d close, and rw.

Continue until you have five rings and four chains.

**Step 8: Complete the Flower**

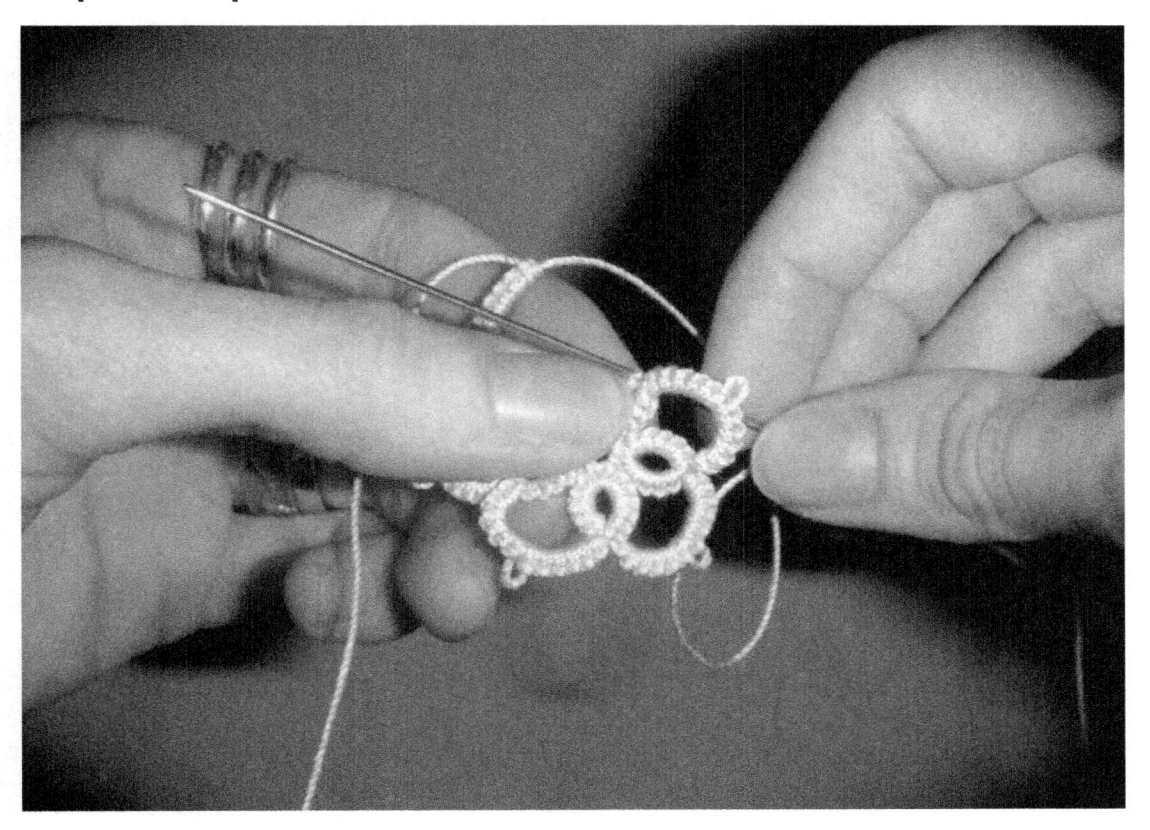

Make the final chain in the same manner, but after closing, connect it to the first ring by passing the needle through the knot.

Finish by tying a double knot and trimming the thread off the ball, leaving enough of a tail to conceal. To conceal each end, pass the needle through a few stitches in the closest ring or chain and draw the thread through. Cut off the excess.

Adding a jump ring to one of the outer picots transforms the blossom into a pendant.

This basic pattern may be made in any color or size, and the outer picots of the flowers can be joined to form chains or embellished with seed beads.

# CHAPTER NINE TATTED-WINGED ANGEL

Introduction: Tatted-Winged Angel

I used some crochet cotton and beads from an old belt to create these angels. They came out pretty good, in my opinion. Although they were created as Christmas ornaments, they can also be used to adorn other objects.

This is an excellent starter project because it is so little.

**Step 1: Resources**

Body jewelry beads

pins with at least a 2-inch head

plyers with a round nose

Shuttle tatting (or tatting needle)

Crochet cotton No. 10 (or whatever you have on hand)

Glue stick

**Step 2: Body White glue Paintbrush Straight pins**

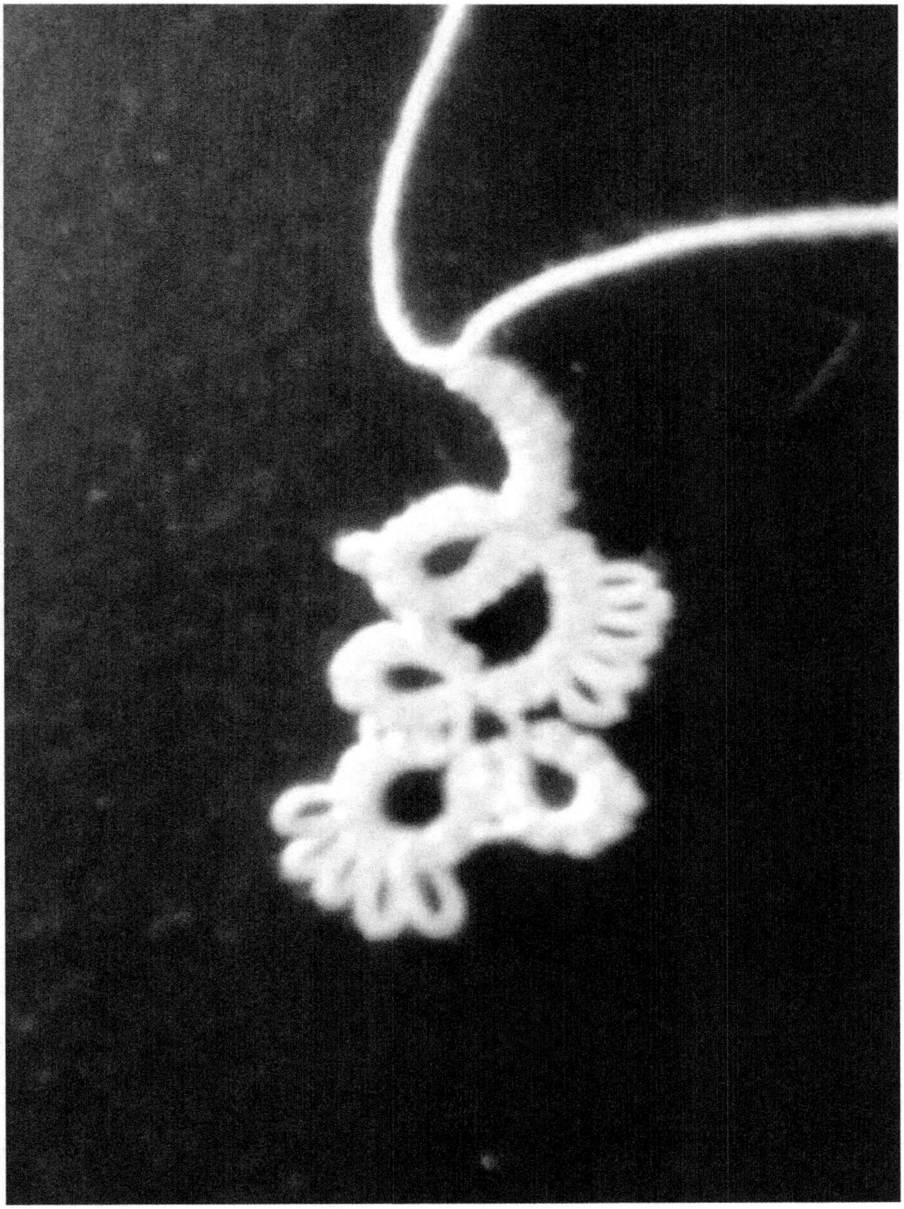

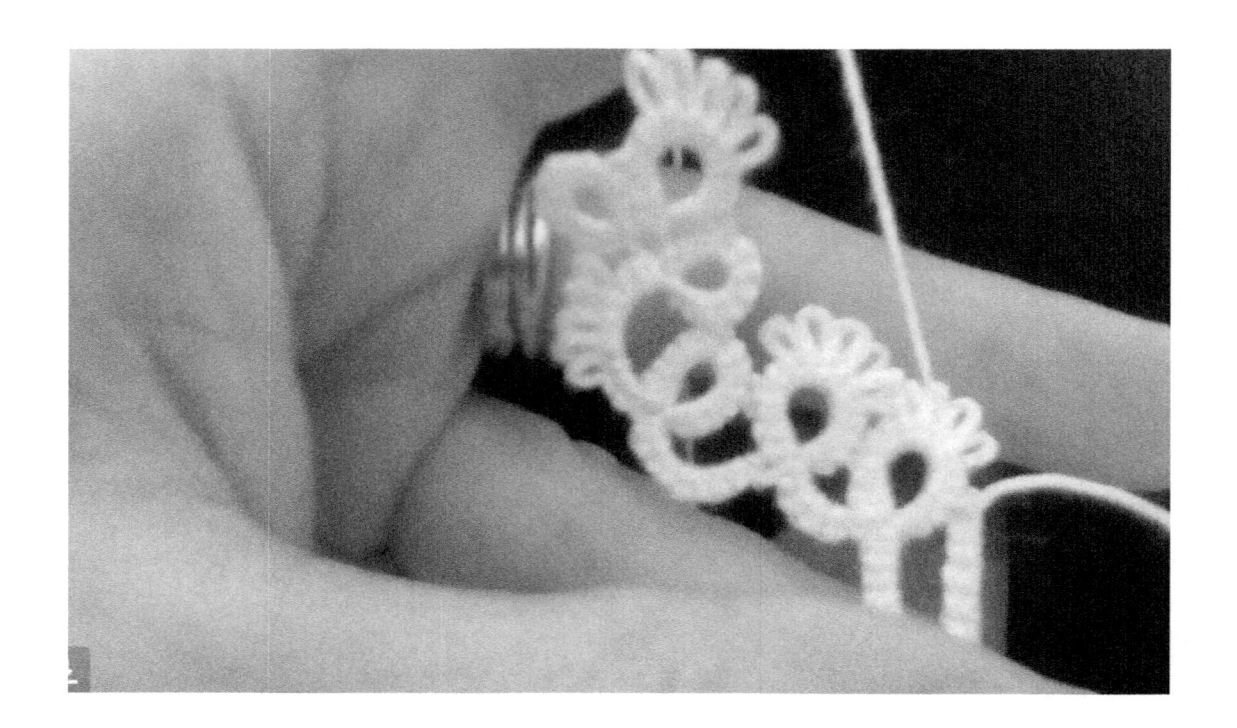

Making the body comes first because I want the wings to be the right size for the body.

I made use of some beads from a detestably ugly antique belt. I disassembled it and discovered that the beads were lovely. As haloes, I used flat gold beads. For the heads, I had some simple wood beads.

After they were strung, I created a hanger loop by curling the head pin's excess wire around the round-nosed plyers.

**3rd step: wings**

The wings are crochetable, but I tatted them. You can find a piece of lace to use as the wings if you lack the tatting or crocheting skills.

The pattern I devised was really simple. I created a couple versions, but this is the one I preferred:

9 dh, 1 p, 3 dh, shut the first ring.

Ring 2: link to the last p, 3 dh, 9 p, 1 p, 3 dh, and then close the ring.

Ring 3: 3 dh, last p join, 3 dh, 3 p, 3 dh, 1 p, 3 dh, close ring

3 dh, 5 p, 3 dh in a chain

Ring 4: 3 dh, 1 p, 6 dh, link to final p, close ring.

10 dh chain

Ring 5: link to the last p, 3 dh, 3 p, 3 dh, 5 p, 3 dh, 1 p, 3 dh, close ring.

5 dh chain (center)

Ring 5 again on ring 6

10 dh chain

Repeat round 4 in ring 7.

3 dh, 5 p, 3 dh in a chain

Ring 3 again on ring 8.

repeat ring 2 on ring 9.

Ring 10: Three dhs, the last p, and nine dhs to close the ring.

Trim and fasten the tails.

Note: P stands for picot, while DH is for double hitch.

**4. Attach the wings.**

Attach the wings to the body's center using super glue. The back is whichever side you stick them to. Super Glue Gel is what I use since it adheres better. I would probably locate another strong sort of adhesive if you only have the thin super glue. It takes a bit for the gel to dry.

**Step 5: Making the Wings Stiff**

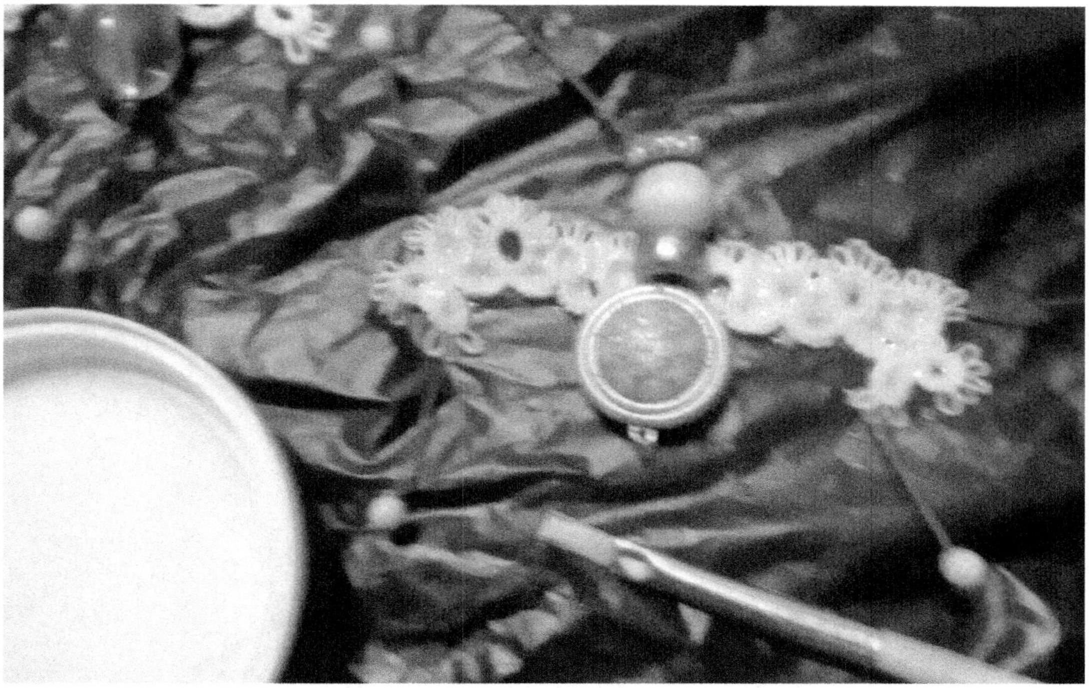

It actually doesn't matter if you are accurate when you combine white glue and water.

Put plastic over the ironing board (or other surface that can be pinned). I made use of a grocery store bag.

Straight pins are used to affix the wings to the ironing board.

Paint the wings with the glue/water combination. Gently blot with a tissue after allowing the liquid to permeate the fibers for a few minutes. This will both eliminate extra liquid from the lace and push a little bit more liquid into the fibers. A small layer of dried glue may form in the midst of the rings if the liquid filler is left there, which could be seen in the finished angel.

Permit to dry. If you want the wings to be a bit stiffer, paint a second coat.

## CHAPTER TEN **NEEDLE TATTING PATTERN**

We have various patterns if you already tat or wish to learn!

## 1. Patterns for needle tatting

Tatting can be done on a needle in addition to the usual shuttle. To help you understand the fundamentals of this technique, Ladybug Lines provides a free tutorial on needle tatting. One of the needle tatting patterns she describes in this tutorial is one she offers for sale in her own shop.

## 2. Necklace with ripple tassels

Basic stitches like chains, picots, and tat rings are used in this lovely necklace. The finished piece is about 17" long, and the tatted portion is around 7" long. Getting the precise curve to match a T-shirt neckline is the trickiest element of the pattern, but it doesn't have to be flawless!

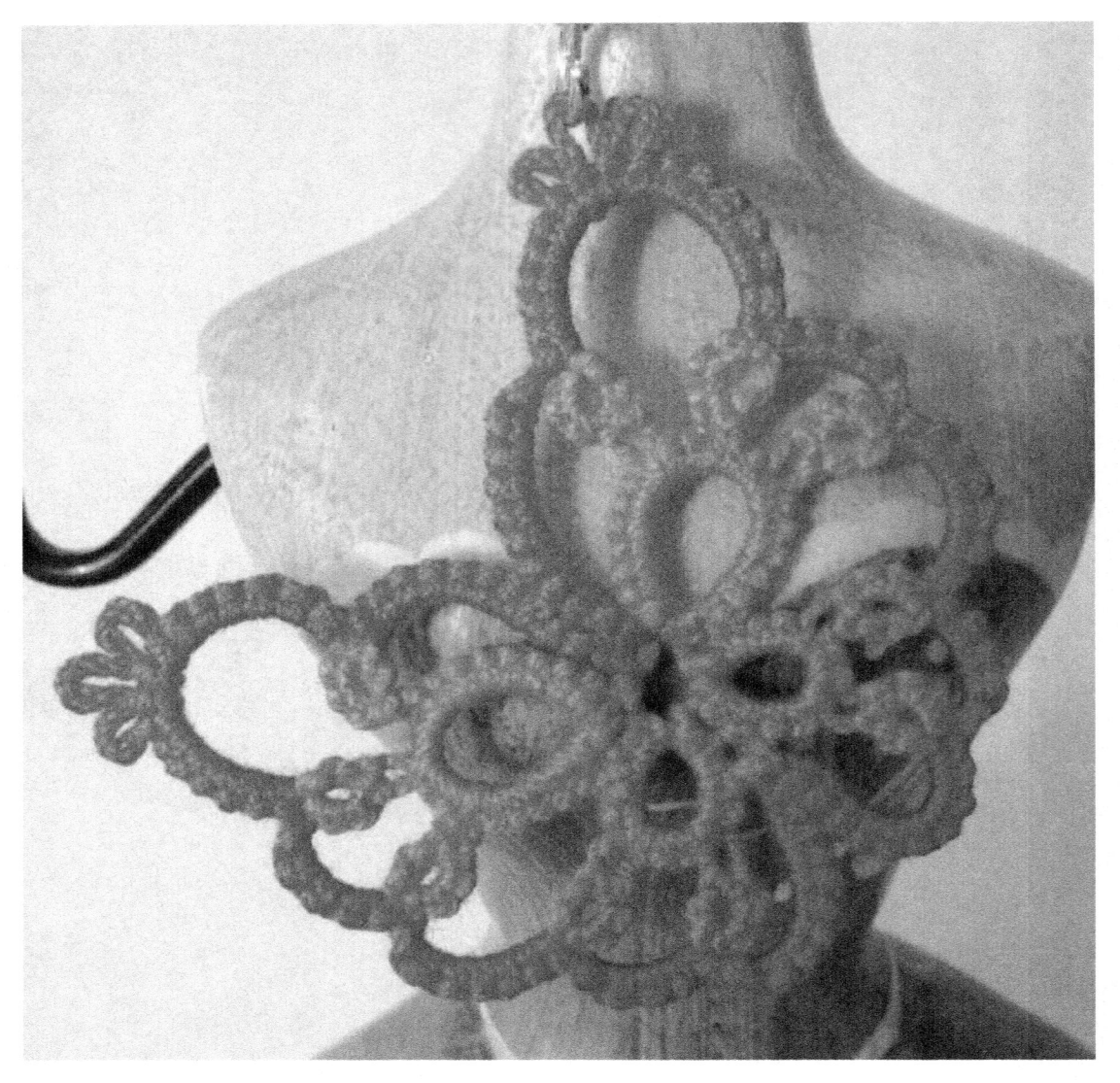

## 3. A butterfly tattoo

This lovely butterfly is one of several reasonably priced tatting designs offered by designer Ororo. It can serve as a foundation for a piece of tatted jewelry or as an appliqué. Work it in a single color for a simpler design or in the two vibrant hues as shown.

## 4. Tatted Necklace

The pendant seen here can be made using the same pattern, and matching earrings can be made using the same colors or complementary hues. Simple beading gives the straightforward design a touch of quirkiness.

## 5. Pendant with a heart design

The beads were worked on the outside of the pendant in the previous pendant pattern. In this one, they serve as the piece's focal point. This is a free pattern from Tattingbox, which provides a variety of enjoyable to discover and use tatting patterns.

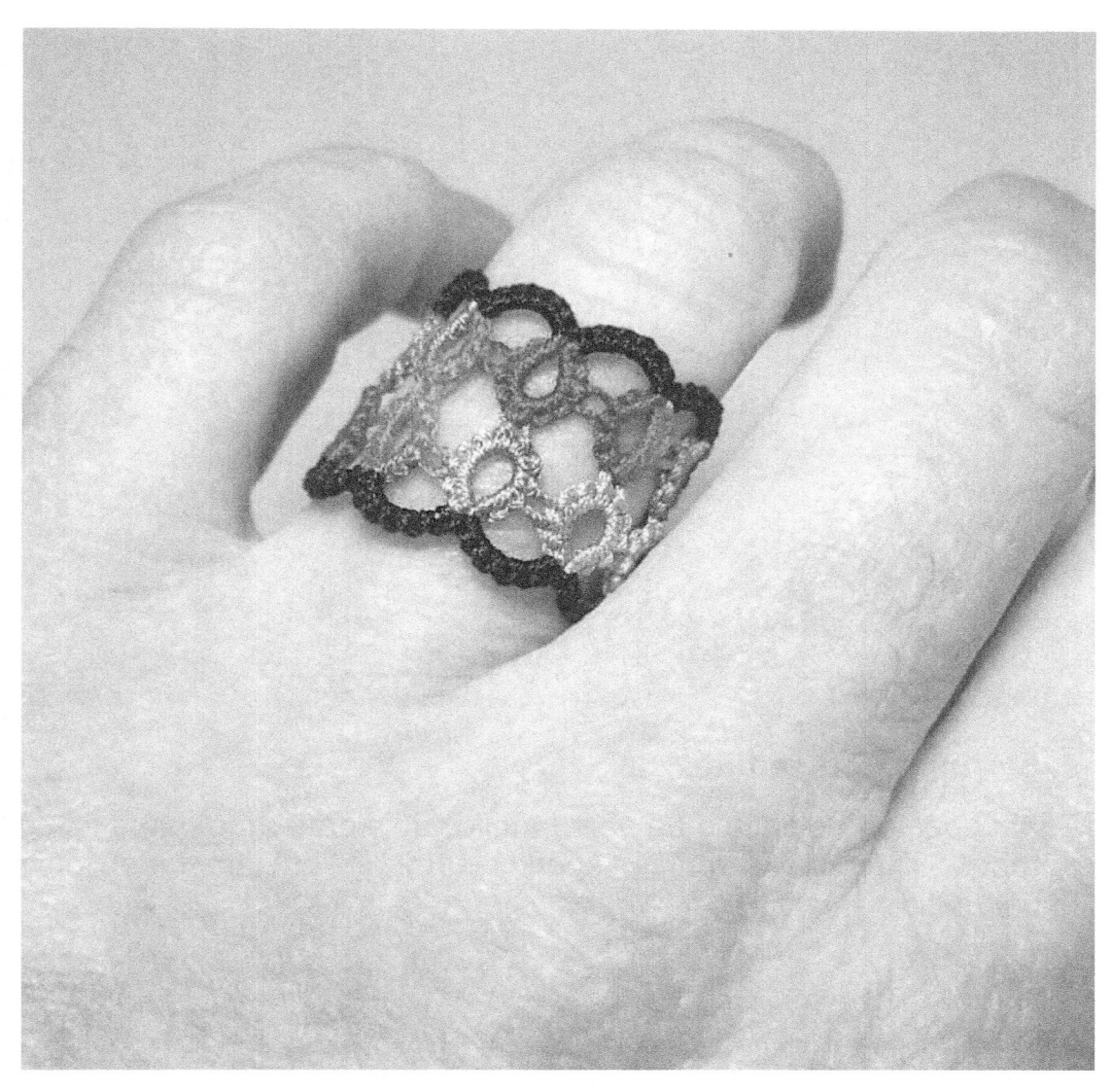

## 6. Commemoration Inked Ring

This fundamental tatted ring pattern uses chains and rings and calls for joining skills. Despite being so basic, this accessory makes a statement because tatting is less popular than other needlework.

## 7. Earrings with Tatting

Tatting beginners should be able to follow this pattern to make these earrings. They are stunning, sparkly earrings that are ideal for a bridal outfit!

## 8. Free Comb Tatting Pattern

Another tatting pattern that would be suitable for a bridal accessory is this one, though it may also be utilized for a variety of other tasks. The free tatted flower pattern is intended to embellish a hair comb, but it can also be applied as an appliqué to other crafts or as a motif for jewelry.

**Flask Cover 9.**

It can be a lot of fun to modernize a traditional craft like tatting by using it to manufacture distinctive objects like this gorgeous flask cover.

## 10. Crocheted and Tatted Doilies

Both the original and replica versions of numerous historical tatting patterns are available. Doilies Crocheted and Tatted, a 1940s antique pattern book reproduction offered by Craftsy user VintageBox, includes 15 crochet doily patterns as well as two tatted doily patterns.

**fake tatting designs**

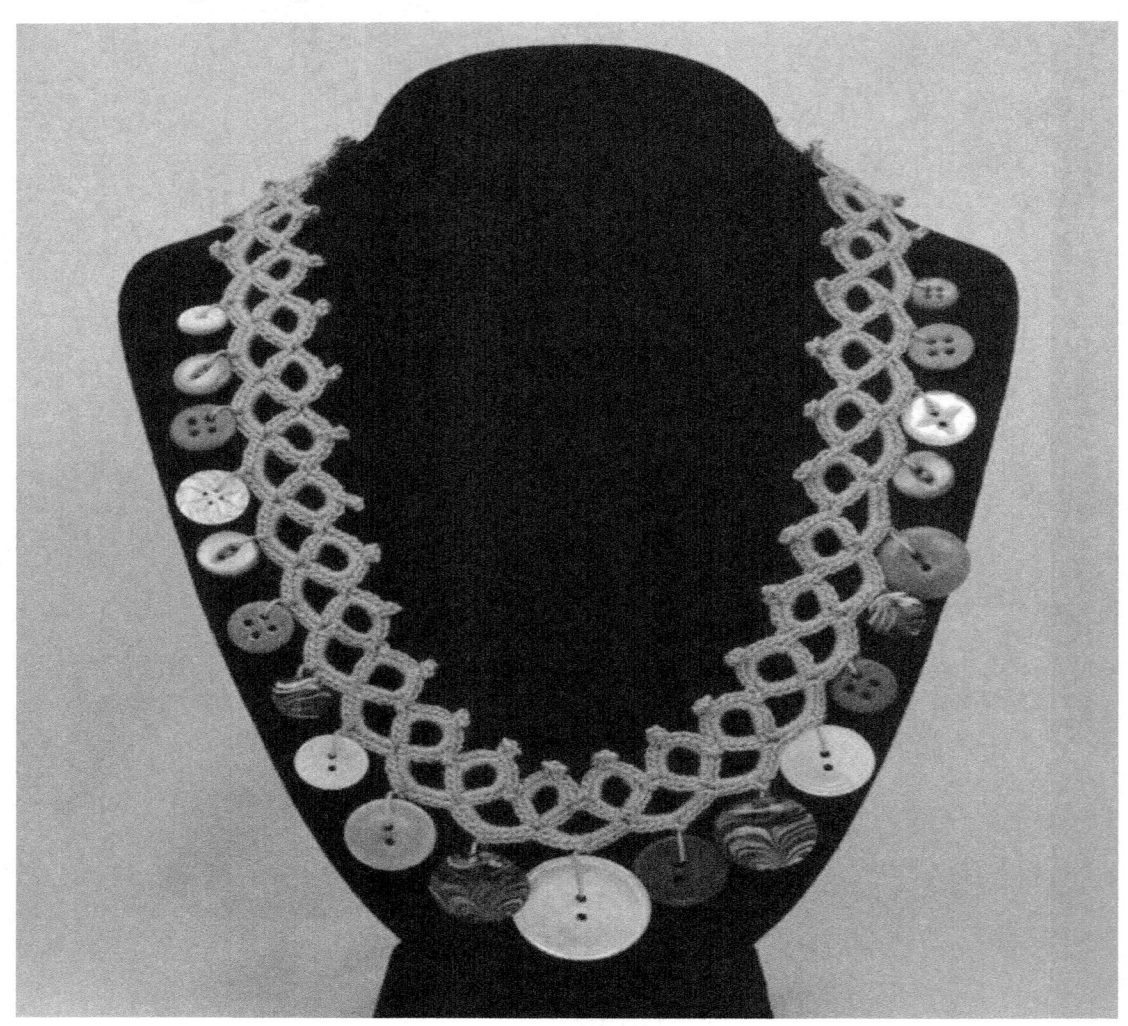

**END**

Printed in Dunstable, United Kingdom